Ruth ~~~~ Nov. - 1949

W9-CEC-316

WITHDRAWN
FROM
UNIVERSITY OF PENNSYLVANIA
LIBRARIES

THE DYNAMICS OF SUPERVISION
UNDER
FUNCTIONAL CONTROLS

**A Professional Process
in Social Casework**

The Dynamics of Supervision

under

Functional Controls

A PROFESSIONAL PROCESS IN SOCIAL CASEWORK

by

VIRGINIA P. ROBINSON

UNIVERSITY OF PENNSYLVANIA PRESS

Philadelphia

1949

Copyright 1949
UNIVERSITY OF PENNSYLVANIA PRESS

Manufactured in the United States of America

LONDON: GEOFFREY CUMBERLEGE
OXFORD UNIVERSITY PRESS

Space and Time

The man looks at the mountain with the fog
of distance on it lovelier than grass
and then he lifts and slowly turns the glass
that calls it to him like a faithful dog.
Man is an animal at home in space;
the earth and sky are beautiful to him;
imagination presses at the rim
of all horizon for a farther place.

He fits his wings to climb as eagles climb;
he fetches constellations in a mirror
but time escapes him; time is unleashed terror;
he is an animal obsessed by time.
He has no instrument to hold it with
except his counted pulse, his measured breath.

—Edith Henrich

From *The Quiet Center*, 1946. Quoted by permission of the publishers,
William Sloane Associates, New York.

PREFACE

Twelve years have elapsed since the publication of my first effort to define supervision in social casework practice.[1] While many articles describing supervisory practice in different fields and agencies have appeared during this period in professional magazines, only one other book has been added to the literature.[2]

In these twelve years I have clarified the preliminary statement of the meaning and nature of supervision in social casework which I formulated in my book in 1936. When I undertook to describe the supervisory process at that time, social work itself was only beginning to distinguish the professional bases and limits in relationships as they emerged out of their personal sources. At the level of understanding of the connection between the personal and the professional, which I had reached at that time, it was necessary for me to hold fast to the early biological relationships through which the individual moves to differentiation of a self as the source in which all psychological growth and professional development must be rooted. I have learned nothing from subsequent experience and thinking to change in any fundamental way this comprehension of the process of individuation in early relationships. But my experience in working with the professional function of supervision in these twelve years, in teaching its use in class and in individual conference, in supervising staff members for whose work I was responsible, in advising supervisors of students in training, has enabled me to lift my description of the process of supervision out of its connection with its early biological and personal roots to a description of a process in itself, with its own characteristic function and dynamics.

[1] *Supervision in Social Case Work.*
[2] Bertha Reynolds, *Learning and Teaching in the Practice of Social Work.*

Because of this new point of orientation, this present book is not a revision or a restatement of my earlier publication, but rather begins where that book left off. I shall not repeat my concept of the learning process as I developed it in 1936 but shall examine the use of that process as I have watched it work in the professional school and in social casework agencies in twelve years of experience.

As I face the difficult task I have set myself, I am struck by two singularly outstanding facts, seemingly antithetical. On the one hand, I am impressed by the amazing efficiency and reliability of supervision as teaching method. I am convinced there is no other method whereby the understanding and skill necessary for social casework can be taught. Against this conviction which prevails in the field as well, I must set the fact that each individual supervisor brings to the use of this function a deep and natural aversion to what is required in the supervisory relationship with another person. Typically, in my teaching experience, I have watched groups of supervisors in class or institute who may have had substantial agency experience in supervising, but who have not at any time been held to a fundamental examination of their own part in the process, quail before the realization of the supervisor's responsibility when they are faced with it in the record of a professionally defined training process.

Supervision, from my point of view, is the most original and characteristic process that the field of social casework has developed. Its use of relationship is rooted in the deepest human sources, its movement follows universal psychological laws. Its effectiveness in the production of personality change, essential for the achievement of skill in the helping process, is undeniable. With all this, perhaps precisely because of it, supervision is instinctively felt to be a dangerous tool, asking more, it may be, of a supervisor to use it responsibly than he is able or willing to take upon himself.

Throughout this book I have endeavored to hold these two contradictory facts in constant juxtaposition believing that in

this conflict lies the essential dilemma of social casework, a
dilemma which can never be resolved but can only be understood and accepted as inherent in all relationship process
which undertakes to become conscious and professionally
responsible.

V. P. R.

Ames Hill
West Brattleboro, Vermont
August 1948

ACKNOWLEDGMENTS

My thanks are due first to the faculty, supervisors, and students of the Pennsylvania School of Social Work who have created the process I describe. In particular to Jessie Taft, without whose contribution to the point of view, to the content, and to the editing of the manuscript, this volume would never have come to completion. And, finally, to my secretary, Grace Good, for her care in typing the manuscript.

CONTENTS

PART 4

THE GRADUATE IN THE SOCIAL
AGENCY

INTRODUCTION

Within the period between two world wars social casework has achieved the status of a professional practice. Social work has developed a sturdy professional organization, professional journals, training schools numbering around fifty in 1948 in contrast to fourteen in 1919 when the American Association of Schools of Social Work was first organized. It has been recognized by the armed services and has made a contribution to army classification processes, to medical and psychiatric services in army and navy hospitals and clinics, and to the program of the Veterans Administration. Great strides have been made in the past ten years in developing and articulating different functional areas of social casework practice, in family casework, child placing, medical and psychiatric casework, day-nursery service, and most recently in services of various kinds for the returning veteran. Granting all the wide differences that exist in point of view underlying these practices and in the skill with which they are carried out, they are united by a basic intent and purpose and increasingly by a characteristic professional method which has been identified and which can be taught in the professional school. What is basic and generic in this practice, essential and characteristic of social casework alone, is curiously elusive and difficult to define. Yet it must be defined as a preliminary to an examination of supervision which attempts to teach the basic skill in social casework practice.

The organization of a book addressed to supervisors in this field of social casework practice and centered in supervisory practice presents a serious problem. It has seemed to me necessary to begin with an examination of the nature of social casework itself, to describe the basic process which characterizes it, the process which supervision undertakes to teach. In Part I of this book, therefore, I have attempted to show how the helping process of social casework has evolved

1

in use and through what experience it has achieved understanding and control.

In Parts II and III, I have followed in the same chronologi-
cal way the development of supervision as a method of
teaching in this field. To get at the essence of the supervisory
function and what is involved in carrying it through into a
professionally controlled process, I have turned to the professional school where the function and process of supervision have been most consciously and responsibly defined
and used in behalf of students. Throughout this description
of a two-year time-controlled process, I have tried to follow
the supervisor's learning experience, his problems and development, as he moves into acceptance of the function of
supervising. The record material that I have quoted to show
the students' learning movement and what the supervisor
must contribute at different stages of the process to help this
movement eventuate, is selected from the records of many
supervisors of many different students in a variety of functional agencies affiliated with the Pennsylvania School of
Social Work in this enterprise of training students. It is a
great regret to me that I cannot identify these supervisors
by name. This is not possible without at the same time
identifying the students who have a right to anonymity in
their learning struggles.

In Part IV, I have followed the graduate of the training
school into the social agency, the medium in which these
helping processes are sustained, to look at the problems involved in the integration of professional training and supervision into the structure and organization of the social service
agency. I leave this last part necessarily incomplete since it
is only in the further development of the social agency that
these problems will find their solution. This development is
in itself a process on which all the unleashed forces in the
world today impinge.

Part 1
THE NATURE OF SOCIAL CASEWORK

Chapter I

THE DEVELOPMENT OF SOCIAL CASEWORK FROM A PERSONAL TO A PROFESSIONAL SERVICE

What is social casework? Have the community fund drives of the last few years with their red feathers and modern advertising methods made the meaning of this service as clear to the public as is medical or psychiatric service? On the contrary, the public may contribute to help the poor, the sick, the friendless, without understanding any more of the nature of that help than that it is offered by reputable established agencies responsible for collecting and disbursing funds to those in need. Few members of the contributing public would conceive of the service of these agencies as anything they would seek or use themselves. How much does the tax-paying public understand of the nature of the service extended to their clients through the public agencies that operate under the Social Security Act, Aid to Dependent Children, Old Age Assistance, Aid to the Blind, or of General Public Assistance? What is known of the casework service to veterans set up since the last war as an essential part of Veterans Administration?

Those who administer these services to people in need, the social caseworkers themselves, who constitute the staffs of the social agencies, are a small group of highly responsible, professional workers. Professional training is fast becoming a requirement in all agencies except in many of the agencies administering public assistance. Back of the practice of social casework lies a tradition, a history, of less than one hundred years in which the idea of social casework has been gathering meaning in use. The date of the first training course for social workers, 1898, out of which developed the New York School of Philanthropy, may be used to mark the beginning of professional definition and development of this field. Actually, its beginning is more accurately marked by the publication of Mary Richmond's *Social Diagnosis* in 1917 and it is in the period following the First World War, in response to the profound changes in human values and relationships, to the deeper understanding of the individual and his needs opened up in these years, that social casework has found its challenge and its opportunity. Today fifty schools of social work are offering two years of training in social casework. There is a national professional association of social workers, there is professional literature to the extent of perhaps a dozen books in the social casework field, and extensive pamphlet material. *The Journal of Social Casework*, a technical publication, is issued monthly.

If one studies this literature one cannot fail, I believe, to get the conviction that there is something vital, alive, and meaningful in this field, something which has genuine help to offer to individuals in need, despite the confusions, the waste of words and efforts, that are at the same time so apparent in many of its writings. One can only bear with its confusions, the lack of clear professional purpose and direction in the field as a whole, if one is willing to understand it in process, to remember its youth as a profession, to realize that thirty years is a short time indeed to make a beginning in defining a service which, resting on the oldest, most personal bases in human relationships, at the same time aims at something so new, so unique and different in the utilization of relationship.

It is significant that with all that has been said and written about social casework there is no brief and ready-to-use definition one can lay hands on. Nor am I ready to offer a definition that would attempt prematurely to simplify the problems and unify the differences in this field. I shall, on the other hand, attempt to state the nature of its task, to examine the problems it must solve if it is to accomplish this task, and to look at how far it has come, and by what road, in understanding and defining its own unique process. This much is necessary if we are to gain any understanding of supervision, the unique teaching process which has been developed in this field.

One has only to listen for a few minutes to the radio broadcasts in a community fund drive to realize the deep personal sources from which this thing called social casework springs. Every appeal reaches out to touch the wound of human difference, to arouse guilt for what one has of equipment, possession, or opportunity that another lacks, and to mobilize for action the ever ready desire to wipe out or equalize difference. Underneath the superficiality and sentimentality of the words of the appeal lie the fundamental psychological and ethical problems growing out of the inescapable fact that each human being feels himself to be different from his fellows in circumstance and opportunity and in something essentially characteristic of himself as a person. The guilt for this difference no individual ever resolves finally for himself; no government, democratic, fascistic, or communistic, has succeeded in eliminating it for its citizens.

It may well be that the sensitivity to the other person, the response to need, out of which the institution of social work has developed, is more active in a democratic society where the fact of human difference is admitted and acted on in all the structures and processes of governmental organization. It is true at any rate that in the democracy in which we live, the United States, the problems of the person in need have always been consciously felt. Out of this sensitivity and responsibility of each man to his fellow, a persistent effort to respond to his need, to discharge some obligation to him, can be traced through the years, taking organized shape and solidity in many institutional efforts directed toward various problems of society. Within these institutions and agencies financed by individuals, sensitive to need and obligating themselves to meet it, the development of a service to individuals in need, known as social casework, has moved ahead to a professional status beyond that which has been attained in any other country in the world.

However, it was not until the passage of the Social Security Act in 1935, when through the depression years the burden of need had mounted to a weight far beyond the capacity of privately supported agencies to meet, that the obligation was really shifted to the tax-supported sources of government. Today these public agencies recognize, as do the agencies supported by voluntary individual contribution, the essentially individualized professional nature of the help they have to offer to individuals in need. In all these agencies, no matter what the source of support, the practice of social casework is defining itself, is developing skill and competence.

This fact of the institutional support for social casework service is of fundamental significance and importance in shaping the unique character of its professional practice. It was just this step, taken when a group of people decided to come together into a Charity Organization Society to administer relief responsibly as an agency, rather than in individual response to individual need, that marked the beginning of the possibility of creating a professional service out of such purely personal sources. This difference continues today to distinguish the social caseworker, who operates always as a representative of an agency bound by its function and policies, from the doctor, the psychiatrist, or the psychoanalyst who, whatever his institutional connection, operates in his own private office, on his own professional responsibility. The implications of this difference for the training and development of the social caseworker are fundamental.

A third factor which has marked the service of social casework as different from other types of service is that, until recently and only in a few fee-charging situations, there has been no money payment from the client to the agency. In all the ordinary transactions of living through which a man satisfies his needs in the environment around him, there are two well-understood ways of relating. One's personal needs for love and affection, for comfort and support, for differing and fighting, for uniting and separating, are projected on people with needs like one's own. One gives and takes and controls in the coin of personal payment so well accepted, if so poorly handled, in the personal relationships of friendship, of enmity, of love, of marriage and family life. Certain needs can be projected onto objects or tangible, defined professional services. Characteristic of these need relationships is the fact of money payment set by the one who has the object to sell or the service to offer and accepted by the one who comes to buy. True, that into the process of buying an object or a tangible service goes something more than the mere payment of the money value set upon the object or the service. The individual choice, the felt impulse or need in the self, which extends itself out to an object, chooses among several objects, and takes possession of it thereafter for his own use, can be a highly exhilarating and life-giving experience. But the aspect of the process that is emphasized is the money payment which carries the relationship between buyer and seller, stabilizes it, and keeps it within bounds.

Contrast these need relationships, the one kind carried in personal payment, the other stabilized in money payment, with the relationship set up by a social agency where the client comes seeking an answer to need and has not the wherewithal to pay or the accustomed controls of the personal relationships. Often he is asking for money, for food, for shelter, for the basic necessities of life for which all men in our culture expect to pay, or for help in a personal situation which has become intolerable. If self-respect is to be maintained and hopefully to be increased in this experience, in what new coin can payment be made? With this problem social casework has struggled, at first more or less blindly but with increasing consciousness, understanding, and responsibility.

What are the problems of a relationship created by one human being's need of something which he cannot obtain in his accustomed way by his own efforts projected onto another human being. From the moment of birth, when the organism is precipitated into an external and alien environment, it must satisfy organic needs through establishing connections with the environment, with the object which contains the answer to need and always in relation to a person who has some control of the source of need satisfaction. As the organism succeeds in establishing its necessitous connections, the ways in which these are established, the very connections themselves, become specific and necessitous so that any interference with these ways may become as threatening or even more so than the loss of the object satisfaction itself. The baby nursing from breast or bottle, or being taught by mother or nurse to control the processes of elimination, gives evidence of the deeply rooted, intricate nature of the connections between need, its sources of satisfaction, and the inevitable role of the other person in the process of need satisfaction. In this process, the child is patterning, not only his own ways of satisfying and controlling his own needs, but just as exactly and specifically his ways of reacting to need in the other person.

Many individuals who succeed in establishing patterns that serve their organic needs satisfactorily and with a use of the other person which is not too destructive or unacceptable to the other person may go through life without having the consciousness of need break through too painfully and without any necessity for change in the patterns of connection or of control in relation to the physical environment and to the other person. Even the sex need when it arises may find its object so quickly and so characteristically that no fundamental change in the individual's patterns of connection takes place. Other individuals find no such easy and simple connection but seem always conflicted in relation to the object choice, rendered confused, obstinate, or negative by the presence of the other person. Some remain confused and conflicted, never able to find direction or satisfaction. Others may seek satisfaction determinedly with the exercise of a powerful will, accepting as little as possible from the other person, sometimes able to get their own ends only by a negative, destructive relation to the other person, or by controlling others through dependency and assertion of weakness. The way the other person, parent, nurse or relative, handles the child in early relationships is deeply determinative of the way this pattern of control and relationship develops.

Whatever the pattern may be that develops in this early childhood experience, it does not easily bear change and interference in any of its established parts any more than with the ends it seeks or with its time rhythms. Certainly some change takes place in these patterns with natural growth and new experience in relationship but always within the limits and along the lines set up by the original experience.

It may profit the reader who is trying to make a decision as to whether he will enter this field of social casework, if there be such a one who has wandered into the pages of this book, to look into himself to see how he reacts in a need situation, to face himself in imagination with the need for some object or person to which he does not have access, or with the loss of some object or relationship that has become necessary to him. Let him add to this the painful realization that, try as he will, he cannot satisfy this necessitous need in himself, or by any reliance on his own exhausted resources, or by his own unaided efforts. It is precisely this grim and desperate realization of impotence that brings a person to the doors of a social agency which has help to offer in this need situation. If the reader can hold himself further to this identification with the one in need, he will know that one does not go to an agency joyfully, with the hope of solution paramount, but apprehensively, suspiciously, with a mobilization of strength to get what he must have in his own way. Perhaps the reader who has consciously lived through an experience in which he has tried to recover a lost object of need can feel the blind rush of defenses to control the object, the other, through whom satisfaction can come. Perhaps he can then guess the overwhelming feeling of this pressure to ward off and gain control as it attacks that other person.

The day-by-day experience of the social caseworker appointed by an agency to carry out its social purpose consists of impact with just such individual need in its most critical shapes, with hunger and suffering; impact with human weakness and strength projected in confusing forms, one masking under the guise of the other. The very life stream of social casework flows through this sensitivity to need, sustained in the feeling response of human beings who act as caseworkers. The individual who decides to enter this field of service to persons in need will be faced immediately and inevitably with two problems: his own tendency, if he is open and sensitive to the other person, to become involved in the other's need as if it were his own; at the same time his reaction, whether it be resistance or yielding, to the kind of will control or pressure which the other person inevitably exerts on him.

What is asked of the worker who elects to enter this field of social casework is not a sacrifice of sensitivity but rather a deepening of sensitivity to the other person and an extension of the areas of his sensitivity to needs different from his own. But more than this, he must learn to find some detachment in himself, some separation between himself and the other person that can enable him to know and accept himself as different in relation to the need and will of that other. In this acceptance and use of difference lies the essential discipline of social casework as a profession. True, some use of professional difference is a part of the training and

discipline of every professional person, but in no other profession does it constitute to the same degree the very essence
of the discipline without which there is no service. Other
professions have more tangible services to offer: medicine,
its diagnostic skill, effective drugs, hospital care, operations;
law has knowledge and technical advice not in the possession
of the layman. But social casework has had to learn that
even when it has tangible satisfactions of need to offer—
money, an assistance check, a home for a child—the object is
never the right answer, is never the solution of the problem,
or enough in itself as an answer to need. Only if something
can happen in the casework process which enables an individual in need to shift his relation to the need object, to
modify his ways of seeking and controlling it, to find a new
relation to external resources and to his own strength and
weakness in himself, is there any real service rendered.

The choice of this professional field cannot be made by the
young person just out of college, no matter how carefully he
has studied the catalogues of the professional schools, or
how widely he has inquired. The real moment of choice can
only come later when he has had experience in using his good
ability, his fine mind, his sensitivity, his intense desire to be
of help, in actual practice under supervision. When he discovers himself inadequate, perhaps even destructive, in the
way he naturally uses himself with a client, then only is he
ready to make a choice. If the realization of problem in himself, in his own equipment and patterns of relationship,
penetrates deeply enough into his consciousness, then he
may really choose to undergo the change in the self, the
discipline involved in learning how to use himself helpfully.

Here, in this moment of realization of his own problem
and his own need, the student worker can experience most
truly his likeness to the client in their common humanity but
he experiences this now in a way that moves, not in the personal way of identification and the creation of greater likeness, but to the acceptance of difference between himself and

the other. In the first steps he must take here, only the function, policies, and limits of the social agency can provide him with any stable, legitimate basis for acceptance of his right to set himself in any way apart, in difference from, or opposition to, the client's need and control. This conviction of difference can never be sustained as personal difference without guilt and involvement, nor can it be long sustained as professional difference in even the most experienced, skillful worker, without the support and limitation of agency-defined structure and conditions.

When the client comes asking, "Will you help me with the problem of my husband, my child, my job, or myself?" the worker can meet this projection of need with a statement of what the agency he represents has to offer, the conditions and requirements the seeker for help has to meet if he uses the agency, so that the relationship is lifted at once in the very beginning, for both worker and client, out of the depths of personal involvement into which any projection of need is naturally precipitated. It makes possible the initiation of a new kind of relationship, one whose limits and boundaries can be touched, which will involve client and worker in a use of themselves very unlike the way that is natural to them in personal relationships. The movement through such a relationship to its eventuation is without precedent in the previous experience of student-in-training or client. Each will strive unconsciously to make it into something more familiar and natural to him and will inevitably become lost in his old patterns unless there is firm, sure help for the student from someone who has been through this before, who knows its course and its possible outcome—the competent supervisor.

With this brief sketch of the development of social casework from its impulsive sources in the need-to-give to the one in need, to a skilled service extended by a professional caseworker who has undergone change in his use of himself in need situations, the profession of social casework today would be in agreement. There is, however, a marked divergence of point of view and practice within the profession as to the nature of the social casework process and consequently a difference of understanding as to the change which the training process effects and the method and practice of supervision. The school of thought which I have helped to develop and with which I am identified, now known as functional social casework, is the practice I will describe in subsequent chapters.

Chapter II

FUNCTIONAL SOCIAL CASEWORK

A divergence in point of view in the theory and practice of social casework began to make itself apparent in the late twenties and early thirties. It was not easy for this young profession, so conscious of its good intention, its positive will to help others, to admit that difference could exist in its own ranks. For social caseworkers to differ was in itself bad and wrong, not to be tolerated. Only when difference could be frankly recognized and discussed was a more vigorous phase of professional growth initiated.

This difference was at first identified, strangely enough, not with the names of teachers or schools of social work but with the names of two psychoanalysts, Sigmund Freud and Otto Rank, a fact which in itself indicates the reliance which social casework found it necessary to place on something outside its own professional experience. In psychiatry, social casework had discovered a new understanding of human nature. Now, in the early thirties, its practitioners were turning to psychoanalysis, not so much for help in their personal problems, as in behalf of learning greater skill in helping others. Whatever the admixture of reasons for which they sought this psychoanalytic help, it gave them a new experience of themselves, of their own needs and motivations, and a new understanding of the meaning of seeking and taking help which had a profound influence on their own relationships with their clients. In these contacts with psychoanalysis they found also an illuminating philosophy of relationship, a psychology of growth, and conscious, articulated therapeutic method. This is not the place to attempt a description of the fundamental differences in psychology and therapeutic

16

method expressed in the contributions of Freud and Rank.[1] The fact remains that these differences found response in already existing differences in social casework point of view and in turn sharpened and deepened them. As a result the profession of social casework now recognizes a division in its theory and practice into two schools. With the one, which still goes under the name of Freudian, or psychoanalytically oriented social casework, I shall not attempt to deal in any way. The discussion of casework and supervision in this volume will limit itself to the practice that has developed under the Rankian influence now known as functional social casework, a term truly descriptive of a characteristic psychology and method growing out of the experience of the profession itself.

This change of name from "Rankian" to "functional" could only come about in the passage of time through a process of assimilation of all that had been learned from Rank's point of view and a shift in focus from the experience of learning and taking help for the self to a new relation to teaching and giving help to clients. It is interesting and characteristic of Rank's own understanding of differentiation in growth processes that, when the powerful influence which emanated from his therapy, direct personal teaching, and writings began to be assimilated by the faculty and supervisors in the Pennsylvania School of Social Work, where his relation to social casework was most fully expressed, there was no tendency to introduce into casework or supervision any imitation or adaptation of the therapeutic form or method of treatment.[2]

[1] For an analysis of the differences in these two psychological theories in their effect on casework, see the following articles: Grace Marcus, "Some Implications for Case Work of Rank's Psychology," *The Family*, June 1938, and "Family Casework in 1948," *Journal of Social Casework*, July 1948; Jessie Taft, "Review of Rank," *Mental Hygiene*, October 1931 (also published in *Psychoanalytic Review*, October 1931), and her Translator's Introduction to *Will Therapy*, 1935 (republished in Otto Rank, *Will Therapy and Truth and Reality;* Alfred Knopf, 1945).

[2] Only one member of the faculty constitutes an exception to this state-

On the other hand, there began to appear a sharper sense of focus and responsibility developing around specific services or functions of agencies and deeper sensitivity to the feelings and movement of the clients in using those services. Irene Liggett's article entitled "Agency and Child in the Placement Process"[3] was outstanding in these early efforts to describe the conflicted process of seeking help on the part of the client of the child-placing agency, and the vital use of agency structure in making foster-home placement a helpful service to parent and child. Almena Dawley's article "Diagnosis: The Dynamic of Effective Treatment"[4] described this process for the parent seeking help in a child-guidance clinic. My book *Supervision in Social Case Work* analyzed the learning process of students as a process of taking help in relation to the function of supervision.

By 1937, this process of taking and giving help had become sufficiently clear, through the use of various specific functions in its fieldwork agencies, to enable the Pennsylvania School to see this process as a universal helping process. Jessie Taft in her introduction to the first number of the *Journal of Social*

---

ment. Jessie Taft, already a clinical psychologist and a practicing therapist, as well as a supervisor and teacher of social casework practice, made immediate use of her contact with Rank in her own therapeutic practice, but at no time confused the therapeutic function or treatment form with the social casework function and process. No one has done more to clarify the differences between therapy and social casework than she, beginning with her first published work after this contact, *The Dynamics of Therapy* (Macmillan, 1933). In this book she applied the Rankian therapeutic method to the treatment of children and at the same time examined the problems of differentiating casework from therapy. Her later understanding and clarification of these differences are found in all her writings, notably in "Function as the Basis for Development in Social Work Processes," published by the *Newsletter* of the American Association of Psychiatric Social Work, Vol. IX, No. 1, 1939, and in her discussion of Dr. Gomberg's article "Counseling as a Service of the Family Agency" in *Counseling and Protective Service as Family Case Work* (Pennsylvania School of Social Work, 1946), pp. 83-94. See also revised version in *Family Casework and Counseling: A Functional Approach* (University of Pennsylvania Press, 1948), pp. 262-72.

[3] *Journal of Social Work Process* (Pennsylvania School of Social Work), 1937.

[4] *Journal of Social Work Process*, 1937.

Work Process, published by the School in November 1937, states this universal base in these words:

In science the hypothesis, the problem, the experiment, the controlled situation, are only various forms of putting up a man-made limitation to nature, to see what will happen and what characterizes the process. In social work, the limitation with which we operate is necessarily the function with its expression in agency policy, structure, and procedures. Certainly function is never completely static or inflexible, certainly it alters over a period of time in terms of changing social conditions or should alter, but relatively it is the known factor, the comparatively stable, fixed point about which client and worker may move without becoming lost in the movement. Every helping situation is an experiment for the worker and for the client. The worker sets up conditions as found in his agency function and procedure; the client, representing the unknown natural forces, reacts to the limitation as well as to the possible fulfillment inherent in the function, over a period of testing it out. He tries to accept, to reject, to attempt to control, or to modify that function until he finally comes to terms with it enough to define or discover what he wants, if anything, from this situation.[5]

In the ten years that have followed this statement, graduates of the Pennsylvania School of Social Work have demonstrated the applicability of this concept of function and its use in all branches of social casework. Herbert Aptekar's book *Basic Concepts in Social Case Work*[6] has been of great value in setting forth the concepts of functional casework in a form usable by students. Most recently, its application in that difficult, unpromising field of work with promiscuous girls has been described and illustrated by Mazie Rappaport,[7] and its value for the oldest traditional field in this

[5] Jessie Taft, "The Relation of Function to Process in Social Case Work," *Journal of Social Work Process,* 1937. Also reprinted in *Training for Skill in Social Case Work,* pp. 100-116.

[6] University of North Carolina Press, 1941.

[7] "The Possibility of Help for the Prostitute through Functional Case Work in an Authoritative Setting" in Rosa Wessel, Editor, *A Case Work Approach to Sex Delinquents* (Pennsylvania School of Social Work, 1947).

profession, family casework, has been definitely established by M. Robert Gomberg.[8] In the two publications just mentioned and in other earlier ones, there are ample definitions of functional casework and analyses and illustrations of its use in various fields. For a brief, comprehensive, and definitive statement of its point of view and method in contrast to the school of casework which is psychoanalytically oriented, nothing better has been said than is contained in the paper of the late Kenneth L. M. Pray, "A Restatement of the Generic Principles of Social Casework in Practice in 1946," presented at the National Conference of Social Work in San Francisco, in April 1947.[9]

Dr. Taft in her introduction to *Family Casework and Counseling: A Functional Approach*, and in her discussion of Dr. Gomberg's article, and Dr. Gomberg in his article on counseling[10] with the two case records give an authoritative, detailed exposition of functional casework in operation, an analysis of the psychological point of view on which a functional helping process is based and of the laws of its movement within a time structure in an agency situation. These articles also differentiate this point of view and method from psychotherapy and from the social casework theory and method that emanate from a Freudian point of view.

In preparing this book for publication during the summer of 1946, Dr. Taft realized that, while the meaning and nature of help and helping had been taken for granted throughout this book and illustrated specifically, these concepts had nowhere been defined in universal terms. In recognition of the need for a statement of a concept of professional helping, as a generic psychological process underlying all

---

[8] "The Specific Nature of the Family Agency" in *Family Casework and Counseling: A Functional Approach*.

[9] Published in *Journal of Social Casework*, October 1947. Also in *Social Work in a Revolutionary Age and Other Papers* (University of Pennsylvania Press, 1949).

[10] "Counseling as a Service of the Family Agency" in *Family Casework and Counseling: A Functional Approach*.

specific forms of casework as well as psychotherapy, she supplied the following:

I would draw a distinction between what might be called "real" help, by which I mean a realistic meeting of need without hindrance and on its own terms, and *psychological* help whose meaning and value are registered in the very experience of taking help through the medium of a helping person whose difference from the applicant is maintained and becomes effective in the process. To take help in this sense is, we believe, the deepest, most fundamental form of personality change and of learning because it penetrates to the roots of human relationships as they are developed from the beginning in the manifold forms of giving and taking, of relying upon, yet struggling to control, those who supply the answer to urgent need from the mother on. Because the original human need is of necessity placed, not on things but on a person, it sets the pattern of all our later efforts to develop within the self enough integration and self-possession to grant to the "other" his equal right to a self of his own, a self which is not there just to meet our need in our own terms. Perhaps no human being ever gives up completely that first image of the all-giving one who has no self-interest to consider, no desire beyond that which is attuned to our own changing necessity. But if maturity, as a result of psychological growth, has any meaning surely it must relate to the degree of success which has been attained in that unending struggle to develop a strength and integrity that can accept and bear internal need without assuming the obligation of the other to meet it and without exerting pressure upon him to fulfill our requirements regardless of his own desire or willingness.

When a man is brought to the necessity of asking assistance from an outside source because of his own inadequacy, inability, or failure to manage his own affairs, whatever has been faulty in his way of relating to the other will be brought into focus as he tries to find his role as client of a social agency. While he is free to concentrate on his own need and to try to get it satisfied in exactly the way he has planned, he is met in the person of the caseworker by something that is quite unknown to him out of his experience in purely personal relations. He has no personal claim or hold on this worker or this agency, although he may try to establish one, yet she meets his request with a consideration for him, an understanding of what it costs him to ask, that answers to an unmet hunger of which he has probably been unaware. He finds also that this worker is not there just to meet his need but that she represents an agency which has a character of its own, a defined purpose, a service with limitations as well as resources. This applicant, whose request has been received with such respectful and thoughtful consideration, is now faced with the fact that the agency presents a difference which must be taken into account and that to use its service, he must go beyond the pressure for immediate fulfillment to a reëvaluation of his own situation in relation to the service which the agency can give. He may decide that this agency does not have what he requires and go elsewhere but, if he stays, he will have to modify his idea of his need and his determination to have things his way in terms of a new plan or purpose which includes the agency in its difference. This does not take place easily or at once but, if the need is acute, the pressure for fulfillment intense, and the worker skillful in meeting it, the struggle to find a way to use the agency that is right for both can precipitate an experience that goes to the very roots of the client's faulty relationships.

No difference in the other is so painful, so unbearable, as that difference which threatens the satisfaction of a need that seems vital. How then can a client who is forced to ask help, not of a friend but of an impersonal agency, ever find the difference which the agency represents to be anything but intolerable although he may be forced to submit by the urgency of his need? That this experience can be a source of fundamental learning, of actual reorganization of the self with which he comes, is due to the fact that the agency is known, is differentiated, through the medium of his relation to the worker whose human understanding, professional skill, and genuine readiness to help, give to the client increasing awareness and possession of himself as an individual whose right to differ is thoroughly respected. It is this combination of regard for him and his need, together with the worker's affirmation of agency as something which goes beyond her power to alter in his favor, that can break up the client's impulsive or

willful presentation of himself and finally permit a true yielding
to the reality of the situation, the agency's and his own. Not
blind submission to superior force or inner need, but a new willingness to let the other have a part in the giving because that
other has recognized the true nature of the asker, has not tried
to control, although he has refused to be controlled.

This, then, is what I understand to be the essence of the helping process, which can take place as a professionally determined
process only when the helper has developed in his own person a
professional self to which the personal need is subordinated and
by which it is controlled when responsibly engaged with a client
as the human representative of an agency whose purpose and
raison d'être is to give a service so that it will be truly helpful to
the individual who can use it.

With this understanding of the meaning of a helping
process basically accepted, functional social casework must
now struggle with the problem of finding limits for the time
structure within which this process can most effectively
operate. These limits can be realistically determined where
tangible services are offered as in child placing, day care,
protective service, medical social service, relief giving, and
public assistance. In such services as child guidance and
counseling, no such realistic basis exists. Therefore, determination of the time limit must grow either out of a responsibility for the psychological movement of the client in the
process itself such as the psychotherapist accepts or out of a
relatively arbitrary limitation of time based to some extent on
agency necessities.

Dr. Taft summarizes this problem in its present stage in
Family Casework and Counseling: A Functional Approach.
There she suggests the use of an arbitrary time span offered
in advance as an agency-limited and agency-defined service,
and likens the resistance both agencies and practitioners
exhibit to the use of an arbitrary time structure to the "older
fear once experienced by many workers in relation to any

firm definitive utilization of agency function." She goes on to say:

It is apparently very difficult for us to look at time in the same objective and realistic way (as the relief budget) when it becomes not the medium for therapy, individually determined by the therapist who is individually responsible, but the particular service which the agency offers to meet a family relationship problem. Neither agency nor worker needs to take on therapeutic responsibility for the length of time it can offer. Instead, on the basis of its past experience, it can offer what it has found to be a useful length of time for dealing with certain kinds of family problems. There is a practical element in this arbitrary limiting of time, just as there is in the limiting of a budget. It should represent what the agency can afford to give in terms of the available time of its workers and the needs of other services. What we evidently fear to trust is the capacity of a client to make his own best use of the time offered, if he can accept its limitation in advance, indeed can choose it as something impersonal and a general policy of agency and not the decision of an individual worker for his case. Although we have learned that clients are helped through the very process of finding and asserting themselves, in the struggle with the agency's conditions and limitations, even in the instance of learning to use a far from ideal budget, or to accept the visiting restrictions of a foster care agency, we still do not believe, apparently, that the client is equally capable of wrestling with, and creating on, the very limitation that a definite time-span imposes. In my opinion, the agency's authority for a time-limited service, even more than its setting of a fee, marks a reliable differentiation between therapy and casework, not only for the client but for the worker.[11]

With this indication of the problems of the use of fee and time limits with which functional social casework is engaged today in its newest, most experimental venture in counseling services, we can leave this brief survey of the development of functional casework. We must ask next what equipment it requires of a worker to practice in this field in this way,

11 *Family Casework and Counseling: A Functional Approach*, p. 270.

to offer the service of a functional agency, to carry a helping process through to an ending with a client, to be a responsible, participating member of the staff of a social agency.

These requirements can be summarized under four headings: First, the worker must have an acceptance of agency as the creator of the helping situation, the whole, greater than himself, of which he must become a part, which limits as well as supports his professional activity. Second, the worker must come to an identification with the function of the agency which from the beginning provides the wedge of separation and differentiation between himself and the client, out of which a professional rather than a personal relationship can develop. Third, the worker must have the ability to enter into this process with the client, to feel and utilize his own reactions as his own while he remains constantly sensitive to the reactions of the client. Dr. Gomberg gives fine accurate expression to the meaning of this participation in the helping process when he says:

I believe that the true power of the relationship as a possible source of help for the client does not lie in the ability to piece together intellectually the meaning of earlier experiences, so that one thus understands the genesis of a problem, important and useful as this may be for the *worker*. *Help* for the *client* rests in the vitality of the immediate contact as an emotional experience, in which the worker takes full responsibility for his own realness and that of the agency. He does not exist outside the sphere of the client's life and conflict, merely understanding, interpreting, and guiding, but rather for the time of the contact he takes responsibility for becoming a part of the client's emotional life experience.[12]

Finally, to practice functional casework skillfully, the worker must have an acceptance of the time-limited nature of the process and some experience with the movement of taking help as it develops in a limited time structure.

[12] "Counseling as a Service of the Family Agency," in *Family Casework and Counseling: A Functional Approach*, pp. 197-98.

Obviously, no purely intellectual learning can give the worker the understanding of this relationship process and the ability to use himself in it. Only an experience of his own, similar to the experience of a client in taking professional help in a time-limited structure and the spontaneity and discipline in the use of himself which eventuate from that experience, can enable him to function as a responsible practitioner of social work. It will be the purpose of the rest of this book to show how this can take place in a training process and to analyze the role of supervision in this process.

PART 2

SUPERVISION AS TEACHING METHOD IN SOCIAL CASEWORK

Chapter III

THE DEVELOPMENT OF SUPERVISION IN SOCIAL CASEWORK

Supervision, with its literal meaning "to oversee, to watch the work of another with responsibility for its quality," has in practice taken on itself the additional responsibility of teaching the learner the skill required. In every field of work —in the crafts, the arts, the professions—supervision has evolved its own peculiar method appropriate to the field and the nature of the skill it teaches and supervises. In industry today, supervision derives from administration and management as a method of inducting workers into the organization, of teaching them the skills and processes they must perform, of holding them to standard performance in time and quality. It is through supervision that the quality of the product is tested and assured. In the fields of education and nursing, supervision has evolved as a means of training nurses and teachers, of standardizing the service of hospitals, public-health nursing agency or school, by maintaining a continuing supervisory control over the quality of service offered.

In those professions where service is offered by the individual practitioner rather than under the control of the institution, as is the case in medicine and law, supervision has not developed to the extent that it has in institutionalized services. Even in hospital and clinic service, the chief of staff, teacher though he may be, does not carry true supervisory responsibility for the internes or young doctors who must learn from his demonstrations, as does the chief nurse on the ward for her nurses in training. The practice of law has developed through an apprentice method of training in which the young lawyer learns in the office and through association with the older, experienced lawyer who takes a paternal or teacher's interest in the young learner, but not the continuous supervisory responsibility as the practice of nursing, for instance, understands it.[1]

During the war, the public had the opportunity of becoming acquainted with several types of supervision developing along different lines appropriate to the particular organization within which it functioned. In the army, where a huge organization is trained and made effective as a fighting force by lines of authority reaching down into small units, supervision develops at every level of authority and responsibility as a method of training, overseeing, and directing the work of the men under supervision. In the air corps, with its smaller units set apart in plane or bomber necessitating a more immediate responsibility for the mission carried by all members of the crew, an entirely different type of relationship and of supervisory control was developed.[2]

In the field of social casework, as in other fields, supervision has evolved in response to the development of the practice in this field and to the agency situation which controls and directs that practice. Since supervision in social casework teaches a helping process, it must itself be a helping process so that the student experiences in his relation to his supervisor a process similar to the one he must learn to use with his client.

Historically, the development of supervision in social casework was slow and at first unconscious. As agencies grew beyond the original staff of one or two workers and new workers had to be inducted, training by apprenticeship evolved as a first step in professional education, bringing

[1] For a vivid description of the paternalistic method of inducting young students into the practice of law in the eighties, see George Wharton Pepper's autobiography, *Philadelphia Lawyer* (Lippincott, 1944), pp. 46-47.

[2] Steinbeck's account of this in *Bombs Away* (written for the U.S. Army Air Force; Viking Press, 1942) is a classic description of the way in which the service and the situation in which it develops determine supervisory method.

with it naturally a certain kind of supervisory responsibility carried by the experienced worker for the beginner. A next step in the development of professional education followed when agencies pooled their resources and sent their new workers to lectures on social problems and methods in the practice of casework taught by the executives of the agencies. At first only a few hours a week were spent in these lectures and classes, the meager beginnings of the curriculum of the professional school of social work, while the real business of training the worker in practice remained with the supervisor, herself without training but with competence gained by experience in the performance of the job. The agency as a whole was actually the training situation in which new workers took on the attitudes of the executives and older workers, became identified with their goals and purposes, and adopted their methods of work as far as it was possible. The very nature of the day-by-day job and service of the agency, helping people in need, tended to bring its workers together in intimate personal association where likeness was at a premium and natural relationships of the character of family relationships were fostered. The small size of the agency, or of the district office of the family society with only three or four workers at the most, was an important factor in the development of this pattern. There was nothing in these situations, in either the nature of the service or the relation of staff members to the agency as a whole, to encourage the use of the authority with which the function of supervision has been endowed in other fields. Responsibility for the cost of the service, for its financial support, for the relationships to its board and to the community which might have furnished the limits out of which acceptance of authority for supervision rightly develops, tended to be left on the shoulders of the executive. This split of the administrative function from the agency's real job of helping clients left the supervisor, who was originally a caseworker herself, identified with the client and the worker in the casework process and separated from the authority inherent in an effective supervisory function.

The stimulus of the professional school and the authority inherent in its teaching function were necessary in order to lift supervision out of its complete identification with case-work and the worker and enable it to take over the authority and responsibility it must accept in order to fulfill its teaching function. It has not yet fully accepted the authority which belongs to its function deriving from its relation to administration and to agency as a whole.

A different development of the supervisory function and responsibility can be observed in the public social agencies where the large, hastily recruited staffs necessary to handle the overwhelming needs of the unemployed in 1929-30 called for a form of organization held together by supervisors who could assume heavy administrative responsibility while at the same time they supervised the workers in the processes of establishing eligibility and getting relief to thousands of clients. A typical supervisory load in the days of the depression might be from six to ten workers, each worker carrying from one hundred to several hundred cases. Final responsibility for the relief check, as well as for helping the worker to learn how to meet her client and assist him to establish his eligibility for relief, fell upon the supervisor.

The problem of developing any kind of professional helping service in these relief agencies at the height of the depression seemed almost insuperable. The workers were untrained and in many cases close to the client group; frequently they themselves had suffered from a depression which was no respecter of persons. The meager relief check aroused intense negative feeling in the worker in his identification with the client. In the supervisor alone was there any hope for the development of enough detachment and separation from the client to furnish a basis for offering a professional service. Since these supervisors were in most instances recruited from the private social agencies, they brought to this public job the determination to try to offer an individualized service even to the overwhelming mass of individuals in need. In the small district of the family agency which constituted a common background of experience for many of these supervisors, they had known the community and the families they served. There they could expect to know all the cases carried by their workers; frequently they had carried some of these families themselves. Transferred suddenly to the public agency, these supervisors found themselves responsible for from six to ten workers, each carrying several hundred cases. It was impossible to know those client families directly or even by record reading. Some way of discharging the responsibility vested in the function of supervision had to be found other than by the way of knowledge of the case load itself. Here for the first time in social casework was exerted the pressure of a responsibility out of which a new orientation to supervision and a more professional process could develop. The necessity of training workers and supervisors to meet the demands of this job brought the professional school into the field at this point to claim a professional service and to lift both casework and supervision out of the routine, mechanical job into which they can so easily deteriorate, to the high quality of professional service they have actually developed.

The first efforts to develop supervision as a technical process in its own right began very tentatively in professional schools by bringing together groups of supervisors from different fieldwork agencies to discuss the problems of student training with the teachers and advisers in the professional school. These discussions continued on the assumption that training was a joint enterprise in which agency, supervisors, and school were equally responsible—a natural enough assumption since the student spent more than half of his time in the fieldwork agency. Only when the professional school moved clearly into its position of responsibility for the student's learning and his training movement was it able to clarify the role of the fieldwork supervisor in its partial place in the total process. Only then could the school take leadership in developing supervision as a technical process in classes taught by members of the school faculty rather than in group discussion with leadership developing where it might.

The first classes in supervision were offered at the Pennsylvania School of Social Work in 1934-35, in the Smith School of Social Work shortly after. Others followed rapidly. A small body of literature has developed, including two books and several pamphlets and articles on supervision published in the technical journals. Very little recorded material of supervisory conferences is available for study. The Pennsylvania School of Social Work library contains some ten or twelve valuable theses on supervisory problems but these are not in print and cannot be made generally available.[3] From my experience in working with supervisors and teaching classes in supervision, it is my belief that skill and competence in the possession of supervisors goes far beyond what the meager published literature would indicate. It is to be hoped that the next decade will bring a development of this literature.

In my book published in 1936, I defined supervision as "an educational process in which a person with a certain equipment of knowledge and skill takes responsibility for training a person with less equipment. . . . In the field of social casework, this teaching process is carried by a succession of conference discussions between the supervisor and the student."[4] To this definition of 1936, a decade of training experience in the use of functional supervision has contributed one revolutionary change. It has clarified the understanding of a time structure with a beginning, focus,

_____
[3] For a selected list of published literature and Pennsylvania School of Social Work theses, see Bibliography.
[4] *Supervision in Social Case Work*, p. 53.

and ending, and its utilization for the movement of a relationship process. This difference between a "succession of conference discussions" and a time-structured process is crucial.

Nothing has been more effective in bringing out an understanding of the learning movement in the student than the use of the arbitrary time form in the hands of the professional school—the two-year training program, structuralized into fifteen-week semesters. This movement begins with the student's choice of the field and the particular school in the application process, proceeds into his use of each part of the prescribed curriculum, until it comes to an eventuation in his thesis statement of his learning and conviction presented from his own practice. From the beginning to the end of this two-year training process, the Pennsylvania School maintains its focus in the practice of the student, the use the student makes of himself, and his understanding of this use, in other words, in a developing professional self and its expression in professional skill. This emphasis on a focus in the self and its use in a functionally defined helping relationship is wholly new to every student and cannot fail to arouse deep apprehension until there is reached a turning point in the process, a new balance in the self, when the student can feel the focus in his movement as his own rather than as external requirement and pressure from the School.[5]

This description of the professional curriculum in social work as a single training movement focused in the student differentiates this concept of professional training clearly from academic education and professional education in other fields where the focus is lodged in curriculum content. At the same time it must be recognized also that, in this emphasis on the use of an arbitrary time form which derives from the educational institution, the professional school

[5] For a fuller description of the meaning of this movement, see Chapter III, "The Development of a Professional Self," in *Supervision in Social Case Work,* and Chapter I, "The Meaning of Skill," in *Training for Skill in Social Case Work.*

introduces into the practice of supervision in the social agency a more clearly defined and sharply limited time structure calling for greater decisiveness in its use for evaluation of the student's progress than casework and supervision in general practice have as yet accepted.

The question will be raised as to why—if the Pennsylvania School so clearly accepts responsibility for the student's training process as a whole—it does not set up its own field-work situations with supervisors appointed and paid by the School, as is the practice in some schools of social work. I have discussed this question in *Training for Skill in Social Case Work* and quote from it here:

> Our original connection with the agencies offers the obvious historical explanation. But more important is the fact that in using this existing school-agency connection we have learned to value the actual agency experience as an essential element in student training. His field placement gives the student from the beginning a responsibility as a functioning part of an agency offering service to clients, more real than is possible when he is placed in a training district set up and controlled by the School.[6]

The very fact that students have their practice in a variety of agencies, each with its characteristic function and organization different from each other yet alike in their conception of a service agency and a helping process, provides the reality and the richness which students need for their development in this professional field. Students understand that in learning to offer the service of a social agency responsibly they are learning also the professional nature of this service as a typical helping process. Through this conviction, their identification is not limited to the particular social agency or agencies in which they have had their practice but is firmly and soundly established in the profession of social casework. As the Pennsylvania School grows it may become necessary to set up special training situations in the field. If this is done, great care must be taken to secure in

[6] P. 4.

these situations the essential characteristics of the social agency in its extension of a functional service to clients with all its realistic problems of organization and community connections.

Between the professional school and its fieldwork agencies there is a constant flow of students into the agency, of graduates in and out of the agency. This mutual dependence creates a special set of problems, which I will not attempt to examine except in respect to the one problem created by the introduction into the agency of the kind of supervision I am describing, focused in a training movement set up in a rhythmical and clearly limited time form sustained by the School. In the succeeding chapter, I will look at the personal and ethical problems inherent in the supervisory relationship for student and supervisor-in-training. In Part III, I have undertaken to present a detailed description of the way in which this relationship so fraught with personal need can become a reliable professional process of learning, change, and growth when the professional school carries responsibility for the process as a whole and for the training of the supervisor as well as of the student.

CHAPTER IV

THE SUPERVISORY RELATIONSHIP: ITS PERSONAL SOURCES AND FUNCTIONAL CONTROLS

No amount of clarity in the definition of supervision, no statement of its role, its function, or its controls, can eliminate the problems which the very nature of the relationship itself arouses for the student and the new supervisor. The School itself, in its tested experience in using this relationship for students, in introducing the concept of functional difference, in its conviction as to the value of functional limits in determining the ongoing, forward movement in this relationship, seems both to the new supervisor and the student to deny the very problems which the relationship creates. There is, I believe, some truth in their accusations, in that the setting-up of any function that brings out into the open or emphasizes a psychological difference between two human beings is a denial of the unity of connection, of the deepest sources of relationship. I believe that any relationship process, whether it be therapy, supervision, or casework, must inevitably stir those deepest sources of connection in the individual who is using it. Unless the professional person responsible for carrying the helping function, at the same time that he holds to the limits of the function, is also able to feel these sources in himself without denial and without personal involvement, the process will be blocked in its movement or limited in the extent to which it involves the whole self of the other person and permits the change he needs.

In every association between two people which has sufficient depth, continuity, and meaning to be called a relationship, there takes place some exchange between the two individual selves involved, an effort to achieve a new balance in the self. Each puts out something of himself upon the other, tries out his likes or dislikes, ventures an expression of his prejudices, his opinions, or the ideas by which he lives. Sometimes one risks behavior which reveals the bad self that can feel anger, jealousy, resistance, the feelings not permitted recognition in the well-trained "good" self that has been built up in family, school, and social relationships. Along with this inevitable tendency in the self to split up its organization, on the one hand, to free itself of what it needs to be rid of as no longer of a piece with the whole, or perhaps simply as too burdensome, too much, to be contained in the self, on the other hand, to give to the other what is precious and dearly valued, goes an opposite tendency. This tendency may be in exact proportion to the first tendency to project what the self can no longer carry alone. It seeks to take back from the other on whom it has deposited parts of itself something in exchange for what it has given. A subtle psychological process impossible to describe with sufficient fineness goes on in the necessity of each individual in relationship to equalize the exchange, to annihilate the difference between them, to make the other like the self through projection, or the self like the other through identification. Each must struggle to control this process in terms of his own pattern and to his own ends.

This fundamental need in relationship has its sources deep in the relationship in which the child is carried in the mother's body and later nursed at her breast. In the uterus, the growing fetus dominates the relationship for nine months and comes into the world a complete, fully formed organism always with some feeling of its own organic unity, no matter how that unity has been threatened with disruption in the throes of the birth struggle. At the same time there is an equally great sense of loss of unity in the birth struggle as all sources of connection with the mother are cut off and the child must establish connections with the sources of nourishment and other life processes in new ways unknown to him. The mother enters into this moment of isolation and disunity to offer the child a new source of connection whereby he can achieve wholeness again through the partial relationship with her which nursing at the breast provides. This nursing relationship between mother and child in which there is the highest degree of mutuality, of giving and taking, serves as the prototype of all mutuality in later relationship.

No matter how carefully and how considerately the child is weaned from this relationship, no child leaves it wholly of his own accord with what belongs to the mother truly resigned, and all that is his own completely possessed and affirmed. Some struggle of wills between them is necessary to produce the separation essential for the child's growth as an individual and out of this struggle some negative elements, anger and hate, fear and resistance, remain as deposits to reappear in later relationship situations. The positive counterparts remain also where love has been given and taken between mother and child, and the need to experience again this mutuality in living is the most powerful craving in relationship.

In the supervisory relationship in social casework, where two individuals enter into a process set up in a rhythmical time structure, this tendency to mutuality must be understood as the basic fundamental trend. It overrides all the obvious factors of difference which would seem at first glance to take precedence over likeness. True, there is an initial phase when student and supervisor alike must go through some struggle to accept each other in this relationship at all, but once accepted even though superficially, the tendency then to create likeness begins to operate between supervisor and student of different ages, of different sexes, of different races, of different temperaments. It is a common observation that a supervisor's first student seems strangely like herself and is so described. The student, I believe, begins with a more painful consciousness than does the supervisor of the difference between them which he struggles to annihilate in every way familiar to him. For him too, as well as for the supervisor, there must be some thread of likeness on which he can bridge the difference and move into the relationship. He may find this likeness in his own most personal terms. It may be as superficial a thing as the color of the supervisor's eyes or the clothes she wears; it may be almost wholly a projection out of the need of the student rather than the supervisor's quality. It may, on the other hand, arise truly out of a deep and sensitive recognition of some characteristic quality with which the student can identify. However real or unreal it may be, some sense of likeness in the beginning of this relationship is necessary in order that there be a beginning but it must be tested and retested, torn apart and built up again on a more substantial basis, until finally it develops into a reliable professional identification.

Given this natural tendency to identification as an early and necessary phase of the supervisory relationship, it is essential that the supervisor recognize it and the trend to mutuality in the process which grows out of it so inevitably and overwhelmingly, as something she must deal with and control in herself if the movement is to develop into a professional learning process for the student. For the new supervisor this ability to differentiate herself from the student, to check her own natural use of relationship, does not come easily or quickly. For her, too, a learning process, a reorganization of the self, is required which begins with her ability to accept a professional difference from the student.

The phrase "professional difference" is glibly said, taken for granted. How natural and easy to slip by it with evasion or denial of its implications! Present this concept of professional difference to any group of supervisors and watch the inevitable struggle against its implications. Typically the opposition gathers under the banner of democracy and contends for equality in professional relationships. One may answer that equality is indeed an end result, that one hopes that the student will in the course of training and practice attain the skill and the competence which is in the possession of his supervisor. But to start with an assumption of equality is to deny to the student his right to any learning process. Add to this, in answer to protest, all the concrete, real illustration of actual, undeniable difference. Remind these supervisors of their own training, of their years of experience, of their knowledge of the agency, of its policies and procedures, in contrast with the student's inexperience and ignorance. Bring out for them some realization of the responsibility they carry for the agency's work and service, which the student cannot possibly be asked to sustain as they do, and the authority that the school places in their hands for the evaluation of the student's progress.

But this answer and these illustrations of actual factual differences do not reach to the depths of the fundamental human problem which is stirred here by the requirement one is setting up in asking a supervisor to begin to take on herself the role of supervising another person entering the profession, to affirm her functional difference. As teacher of this practice of supervision, one must comprehend the depth of the characteristic human aversion to assuming the role of supervisor and know that there is no escape from the guilt that such an assumption of the right to assert and sustain a difference from another human being arouses in everyone. Even though a caseworker has learned to affirm and use her difference in the role of helper to the client, she cannot move into the role of supervisor and affirm her difference from the student or worker, so much more nearly her equal perhaps than her client, without experiencing new depths in this problem of separation and differentiation.

I know of no more touching and meaningful illustration of this guilt for difference and the problem it can create in a supervisory relationship than in a story told by St. Clair McKelway in his articles on "A Reporter With the B-29's," published by *The New Yorker*.[1] I quote from those articles:

Everybody seemed to realize that everybody else was working his head off. Requests were made, commands were given, in quiet voices. Everybody seemed almost miraculously full of tolerance and understanding.

There was a major who had worked all night in his Quonset office and was about to grab two hours' sleep on his office cot before going on with his work. Around 6 A.M., he telephoned a staff sergeant, a clerk who he knew was on duty in the main administration building of headquarters. The major had to have an envelope that contained certain secret matter. The sealed envelope, with his name on it, was in the headquarters safe. He had to have it, he told me later, in case the information in it was required of him at a conference he was to attend after the nap he was about to take, and he had decided it would be better if he had the envelope in his breast pocket when he took his nap. He wanted to get it into his pocket and off his mind. He called the staff sergeant whose duty it was to look after the safe, to put things in it and take things out for all the officers who used it. The major explained about the envelope and asked the sergeant to get it and bring it over to the Quonset office right away. The staff sergeant, who had been working all night too, asked if he could wait and have the clerk who was to relieve him in about fifteen minutes deliver the envelope. The major said no, that he really wanted the envelope right away, that he hated to ask the sergeant to do it, but would the sergeant please bring the envelope over to him right away? The sergeant started to say something further and the major, a bit tense but still good-tempered, told the sergeant he didn't want to talk about it any more, told the sergeant just to do what he had asked him to do, and then hung up while the sergeant was still talking. Five minutes later the sergeant brought the envelope to the Quonset, saluted, and laid it on the major's desk. Then the sergeant stood back, saluted again, and asked, "May I say something, sir?"

The major sleepily replied, "Sure, sergeant, what is it?" and leaned back in his chair and looked at the sergeant.

"Sir," said the sergeant, "I just want to say that I consider your

1 "A Reporter With the B-29's" by St. Clair McKelway. *The New Yorker*, June 20, 1945, pp. 34-35. Copyright 1945, The F-R. Publishing Corporation. Used by permission.

having hung up on me just now a very rude and unpardonable thing for an officer to do. I work hard and I do my job and I have never been subjected to such treatment before by anybody and I have been in the Army for three and a half years."

"My God, sergeant," the major told me he managed to say, "I'm sorry as hell you're taking what I did that way. I know you're a damn good man, you know I do, and you've helped me out several times before—done work for me you didn't have to do. I apologize, sergeant, for hanging up on you, and I don't want you to think for a moment—even though what I did was wrong—that I meant any lack of respect for you when I did that."

"I consider your having hung up on me sir, the same kind of mistaken thing General Patton did when he slapped that soldier."

The major says he sat there looking at the sergeant and that tears were suddenly in all four eyes in the Quonset office.

"There he stood," the major said, "a middle-aged fellow, a good guy and a good man all through and up and down, and I'm telling you he taught me a lesson and did something to me as he stood there that I'll never forget and that I hope I'll never get over. I didn't know what it was he represented at the time. All I know is that it made me want to shake hands with him and then maybe cut my throat. I've figured out since that he was the dignity of man personified, if you see what I mean. He stood there and I looked at him and I apologized again. And then *he* began to feel bad because he could see that he had somehow hit me below the belt, so there we were, with tears in our eyes, and he wanting now to apologize to me. I'm still a little hazy about how the hell we ever got the thing straightened out. I think he started to apologize to me while I was apologizing to him for the third time and we both laughed and he saluted again and I told him never to lose whatever it was that had made him tell me what he had and he said something about how he hoped I would just forget the whole matter and finally we saluted each other a couple more times and he left and I lay down on my office cot and cried for a second and laughed for sometime and then went right to sleep, feeling wonderful. It's the damnedest experience I ever had, and I thought I had had some in this war."

Here in this brief episode between a major and a sergeant

is personal guilt as it inevitably manifests itself in relationship, deeply felt and sensitively described. Guilt such as this dissipates and confuses the strength of purpose and direction of movement in both individuals. Both are precipitated into personal and ethical questions of debt and responsibility to the other and must handle them personally as best they can. Only the obligation to the common task, the functional difference, can restore clarity and direction to the relationship.

This guilt reaction must be expected to arise again and again in the supervisor who is learning to take on the role of supervisor for the first time and can only be handled as it is honestly faced in feeling. Only when the supervisor has come through a process with a student to an ending where she can clearly see the use the student has made of her functionally defined and sustained difference, will she have in herself the true differentiation and partialization of herself which enable her to supervise with conviction.

While both student and supervisor alike feel the pull toward mutuality which this relationship arouses, the student's struggle against it is very different from the supervisor's. The supervisor has chosen and accepted the role of supervisor, difficult as she may find it to hold to the role in actuality. The student, on the other hand, even though he has chosen training with all the consciousness and will he has to put into a choice, has not yet accepted the role of student, will struggle against it and try to control the relationship in every way. He must oppose the will to teach him which the training situation places on him no matter how much he wants it. He must test the supervisor's strength and his own choice until he is sure it is his. Against the supervisor's assertion of her difference and ability to teach him, he will oppose his effort to make the relationship equal, a social, casual, friendly contact. The use of first names between them, the habit of staff lunch, and the discussion of common interests encourage this effort on the student's part to wipe out the threatening difference. He needs protection from these casual associations which invade the supervisory relationship and the supervisor should find ways to help him avoid them.

One may well wonder what stays this pull to mutuality from drawing the student into a deep personal and therapeutic use of the relationship. It is only the inescapable reality of the function he has chosen in electing the profession of social casework. This function is the helping function which he begins to carry with a client in terms of the agency service from the day he begins his training and enters into a supervisory relationship. There is no preliminary period in which he learns to take help from a supervisor in order that he may later give it. But at one and the same time he must take help in a learning process with his supervisor and give it in a helping process with a client. This training experience asks that the student be both student and helper simultaneously. Seemingly contradictory as this is, the fact that it works in practice is incontrovertible. It is not achieved by the student's deserting his side of the desk and trying to take on by any effort at imitation the supervisor's function and methods. His process must be exactly the opposite. Nor, as might be anticipated, can he derive his strength to act as helper to a client in reliance upon the supervisor's undeviating support. Support there must be for the process throughout, but to his work with the client the supervisor must be able to react with her difference, with criticism. Although this may precipitate the student to the depths of inadequacy in one moment of feeling, he must be able to rally from this guilt and helplessness to an assertion of his role as helper to the client. What he pulls out of a conference in which he comes to awareness of his error or his problem in relation to what he is doing with the client, and what he takes back to the client in his next interview, brings about some partialization and objectification of himself that constitute a beginning of a professional use of the self rather than a merely personal one.

This characteristic of the supervisory relationship, that it is inextricably related to its content, the helping process with the client, requiring of the student a constant partialization of his total impulsive projection of himself, is the greatest protection against the trend to personal and mutual use of the relationship. There is present always the controlling factor that the relationship requires from the beginning the inclusion of a third person, the client.

This three-person relationship is characteristic, not only of supervision, but of the social agency itself in which this three-way process has naturally developed. In addition to the client there may be another worker on the case who must be included in the student's contact. There are agency policies to be considered and other members of the staff. There is also the school, the student-adviser, and his teacher. Everything in the training process, in agency organization and structure, requires that the student who enters this professional field give up something of his own natural, individual relationship to what he is doing to include other realities that have a part in the situation. This necessity to take in the third person, to become a part of a new whole, requires of any individual a deep, new learning.

Those individuals who have never achieved a separation from the first-person relationship with the mother may not be able to accept the partialization which this training asks. Some students take hold of the personal help they feel extended in supervision but cannot rally their strength and difference to take on the function of helper. When it is clear that the student cannot, or will not, move into training but must use the relationship for his own therapy alone, the school must discuss this with the student and refer him to a therapist for the help he needs if he will take it. While he is finding that help, in most cases it is necessary that he should leave professional training in order that he may use therapy to the extent of his personal need. When he has ended that therapeutic experience, if he chooses again to prepare himself for professional casework and can stabilize the will-to-be-a-helper sufficiently, he may attempt to reënter training. The ability of the school to evaluate these problems, to help the student who cannot use training to leave, depends upon its clarity and decisiveness in the use of its own training function.

In concluding this examination of the basic human problems in the supervisory relationship created by the need of both student and supervisor to use this rhythmic time structure for their own personal experience, I want to state again my conviction of the unique opportunity which this relationship can extend for professional learning and development when the relationship is safeguarded for this purpose through the use of functional difference and the responsibility to the common task, the service to the client. At the same time, as I have pointed out, the very assumption on the part of the school of the right to set up and utilize functional difference as the dynamic of movement in the supervisory relationship implies a denial of the trend to mutuality, of the personal sources which feed relationship, of the necessity to create likeness and make a personal utilization of difference in all relationship processes which involve the self deeply. Unless the school retains its sensitivity to these problems and can extend help to its supervisors as well as to its students, it will find itself constantly thwarted in its effort to carry out its training function.

The constant partialization and new organization of the total impulsive self which are in essence the requirement of the training process in social casework are asked for in every aspect of the training situation, in the supervisor-student-client relationship, in the adviser-student-supervisor relationship, in all the parts of the agency-school structure. All exemplify the essential three-way relationship characteristic of reality and necessary for living and for growth, which for all human beings who have accepted any partialization in early experience constitutes the guarantee of the essential naturalness and universality of the professional process as a true growth process.

PART 3

THE SUPERVISORY PROCESS AS DETERMINED BY THE STRUCTURES OF THE PROFESSIONAL SCHOOL

CHAPTER V

THE DIFFERENTIATION OF ROLES BETWEEN SUPERVISOR AND STUDENT

The student entering professional training in the Pennsylvania School of Social Work is told in the catalogue statement and in conference with the application secretary and with his adviser that his fieldwork practice in the agency to which he is assigned will occupy three days a week of his time. He[1] is told and to some degree understands the importance of this practice in his training and the fact that his supervisor in the agency will be the person with whom he works on that practice in regular conferences, the person who will know and evaluate his practice with him and with his adviser in the School as the school year goes on. I say he understands to some degree, for this relationship created by his studentship under supervision is a new one, the actual character of which he cannot possibly comprehend until he has experienced it. He identifies it naturally with earlier relationships experienced in school and college, with the teaching and tutorial relationships which were sustained by content and subject matter, with all the typical student resistances to authority and with their individual and personal manifestations. No modifications in these reactions to authority were expected of him in these former teaching relationships, provided the subject matter was mastered. The good student felt himself at home and adequate in these learning relationships of college.

At the very beginning of his professional training, the supervisory situation is described to him by the adviser and set up by the supervisor with definiteness and clarity as to

[1] Except when particular individuals are referred to, the masculine pronoun is used arbitrarily to designate the student, and the feminine to designate the supervisor in order to keep the distinction clear throughout the book.

time and statement of purpose. There is content offered in the first hour, some picture of the agency, perhaps a case assigned to the student, a visit where he will have a role to perform in the situation definitely planned. He understands that he will make a record of that visit and that it will be read by the supervisor. He knows that he will return to the supervisor for an hour's conference on what he has recorded and with his questions about what he did, about the client's reactions, about next steps. He is told that he should expect her questions. But does he know that, even though she has told him? If he has really got into this new enterprise, he has likely projected his own way of working and controlling to a degree that has already excluded the other person, his supervisor. Or if he has not gone so far as to exclude her, at any rate he can have no idea what she will put into it. Young students fresh from college discipline frequently bring notes and take notes in these early conferences, are surprised and hurt by the suggestion of the supervisor that this formal note-taking may interfere with what they need to get to here. The formal, organized, controlled, businesslike use of conference time seems to them right and proper in contrast with the informal, loose, give-and-take, gossipy exchange of the personal relationship. Of a professional relationship, different from either of these, they have no conception but must learn that difference through experience.

If this learning is actually to take place in supervision, it can only come about by the supervisor's recognition and acceptance of professional difference between herself and the student—any student—as the basic factor on which the relationship begins.

A young caseworker supervising for the first time, and therefore as much a student in relation to this new practice as her student is in relation to casework, has much to do to establish her difference from the student in her own attitudes. She must separate herself from the case load where she is at home in order to help the student find his relation to it. She must sacrifice her own skillful relation to the client and let the student's awkward, bungling relation intervene. She will suffer for the loss to the client which this occasions temporarily, at any rate, and will wonder if the student's professional development is worth the cost. Sometimes she holds onto the case or intervenes to take it out of the student's hands or unwittingly separates him from it by her own interest and superior capacity to handle it. From these tendencies she must be helped to extricate herself by the student's adviser or the casework teacher, whose primary concern is always for the student.

This young supervisor will of necessity have to assert her difference arbitrarily at first and support it by every formality. The limits of the conference hour may have to be rigidly held to, the content of case discussion planned carefully in advance. Only experience can give her ease and flexibility in sustaining her role. The student will engage his will against hers at any point where hers is mobilized rigidly, and he will therefore have more than the usual training resistances to work through. Again the teacher in the School must help with this by her direct contact with the student as well as with the supervisor. Despite these hazards, experience has proved that a young supervisor can give a satisfactory experience to a beginning student if the whole training process is supported firmly and consistently by the School.

When the supervisor has had sufficient experience to be free to rest on and use her function easily and naturally with the student, there is opportunity to examine how the student begins to find his way into the fieldwork and the agency and how he uses her function in his efforts. First of all, it must be recognized that a careful application process in a school of social work brings to this point of fieldwork placement under a supervisor only students with good ability who are accustomed to success in academic work and in whatever jobs they have engaged in.[2] In coming into training for the field of social work, they have made a professional choice which involves them more completely than any previous educational or vocational decision. They have chosen specifically this particular school for various reasons and have had a chance to test the validity of this choice in an application interview. They may know of others, perhaps classmates, college friends, or fellow workers in the agency where they have been employed, who have been rejected. Many bring with them hearsay tales about students who have been rejected after the first semester or have failed to be recommended to continue after a first year. So the typical reaction of eagerness and assurance and the accompanying apprehension with which everyone enters upon a self-chosen new enterprise are deepened and reinforced here by the application process appropriate to the professional training ahead. The student goes to his fieldwork assignment with all the assurance he can muster, glad to have been chosen, ready to get to work. His previous training and education have taught him to deny or to make light of any indications of fear, if indeed he is conscious of any. The idea that he should actually have resistance to beginning anything he wants so much and has chosen so deliberately is foreign to his whole conception of himself and his way of working.

This positive constructive way of beginning may take many students through the application process which, no matter how hard it tries to present what will be involved in professional training, may be powerless through words alone to bring to the student's consciousness any awareness of other underlying attitudes. Classes, too, have the familiarity of the college class for the young student and at first therefore do not stand in the way of his getting to work to master assignments.

The fieldwork agency and the supervisor, on the other

[2] Margaret Bishop, *The Selection and Admission of Students in a School of Social Work.*

hand, present him with a reality which opposes his constructive, outgoing energy. In the first place the fieldwork placement is the choice of the School, not necessarily his own.[3] Even though it may be in the area of his own choice, once the assignment is made, it becomes the School's decision rather than his. He begins to question various things about the agency, to compare his placement with that of other students. Occasionally he will protest it with the adviser; but more typically he will accept it, hiding his criticism and suspicions behind a surface acceptance which asserts that the agency is wonderful and everything is all right.

The supervisor, standing at the very center of this agency experience as he engages with it, becomes for him the focus of his unrecognized suspicions and fears. Sensitive to the difference which she actually carries in her superior experience, knowledge, and skill to which he cannot submit until he has accepted his own reactions to being an ignorant student, he uses any personal difference he can find to carry his criticism or his fear to level her to equality with himself. She is too young; she never had a student before; she is too old; there is a color difference between them, a racial difference, a sex difference; she was trained in a different school. It would take more courage and directness than he possesses to face this criticism with her or with anyone in authority,

[3] The following catalogue statement indicates the extent to which this decision as to field work assignment rests with the School and makes clear what the student has in writing before he begins this training:
"Field Work—First Year
"The student receives individual attention in the arrangement of his assignment to field work, as well as to class section. The selection of a field work placement rests upon a number of factors, and the final decision in the selection rests with the School. Nevertheless, the student's preference is taken into account and he is notified by his faculty adviser of his assignment as to agency at registration time, or before by letter, whenever possible.
"First Year field work placement does not commit the casework student permanently to a particular functional field. Specialization occurs in the Second Year.
"Throughout the First Year, students devote three full working days a week to field work. These days are Mondays, Thursdays and Fridays."
(Pennsylvania School of Social Work, University of Pennsylvania, *Catalogue Issue,* 1947-48, pp. 22-23.)

but in some cases the adviser may sense the attitude behind some tentative question and be able to bring it out in the open for what it is.

For the young supervisor who also has difficulty in accepting her youth and inexperience, it is hard to realize that these factors are not really the cause of the problem the student is feeling and expressing. Yet she can help him get to an awareness of his negative attitudes if she can believe that they are inevitable reactions to this new experience and that they will inevitably be projected onto her person or her professional function. She will have to protect her personal difference and handle her feelings about it as best she can, perhaps needing to talk that over with her own supervisor or with the adviser in the School, but with the student her attitude must be clear, firm, and unequivocal. If she can hold to her professional function and a conviction of the necessary difference it creates between them, she will become increasingly more skillful in helping the student to recognize his attitudes and his projections as his own and to accept himself as a student, a role different from hers, which carries its own rights and obligations as well as its essential limitations.

A supervisor's use of this differentiation in role and her understanding of its meaning for the student in all of its implications in a training process and in the inherent similarity in the relationship between client and student is well illustrated in the conference quoted below. The supervisor has had many years of experience in a child-placing agency and is at home with her supervisory function; the student is young and inexperienced in the field.

At our conference we spent a good deal of time on one interview. I commented on the fact that there was a great deal of movement shown in this interview on the part of both the foster mother and the worker and that I felt both had come a long way in understanding and acceptance of each other, as well as of the part the agency had in this situation. We reviewed the steps which had led up to this interview. I said that, of course, we could not expect the foster mother to maintain this level and there would be many ups and downs, but that a beginning had certainly been made. Student was quite aghast that this level could not be maintained and said, "You mean we are going to keeping working at just this some more?" I said indeed I did, that learning and changing were slow processes and it was a long time before they became parts of one. I asked him if he thought the foster mother was as concerned with Stanley's relationship to the agency as she was with her own. Wasn't that really what she was trying to say to the worker? Student said, "Well, I certainly missed that." I said perhaps he had, but in discussing Stanley's problem, he had got a great deal over to the foster mother and in a way which she could accept.

I said that maybe the student was having some problem himself in really knowing why the agency was going into foster homes and what his relation to the foster mother should be. He denied this at first and then said that it was hard for him to really understand all of it. I said I knew that, and that we only expected him to get it step by step, the same as we did the foster mother. He said, "Oh, you think I'm a client too." I said, "Well, aren't you? What is a client but someone asking for something from the agency. As a student, aren't you asking for something from a school which also might be an agency of its own kind?" He said, "Well, I'll have to think about that." I said that I could understand that and it was only after thinking things through as well as experiencing them that we made them a part of ourselves.

The essential elements which a student needs for his training process are in this supervisor's attitude and brought out in words for his use if he is ready to use them; the unequivocal assertion that he is a student and like a client in that he is asking something from an agency, the School, and from the supervisor, combined with the knowledge that the process is slow, that he, like the client, is expected to get it only step by step in his own experience.

This illustration highlights the problem of the beginning phase of the training process for the student entering a professional school of social work as I have described it in this chapter. The definition of difference between supervisor and student must continue throughout the whole supervisory process and indeed may be said to be the fundamental underlying motif, the necessary condition in the training movement. In these early conferences that mark the beginnings of the relationship between supervisor and student, the definition of the difference in roles may seem crude and arbitrary. In every case, no matter how stated, for the student it amounts simply to the beginning of a realization that he is a student and in that role is, like the client, asking something of the supervisor and the school. When he has accepted this for himself to however slight a degree, his learning has begun.

CHAPTER VI

THE SUPERVISOR'S RESPONSIBILITY FOR BRINGING OUT THE NEGATIVE ELEMENTS IN THE STUDENT'S EARLY REACTION TO SUPERVISION

Criticism is always leveled at the emphasis this School places on the necessity for maintaining the function of supervision in its professional difference from the role of the student and on the inevitable negative reaction of the student to this necessity. This criticism frequently says, "Why make it hard?" and "Isn't learning a positive experience, not a negative one?" The answer to "Why make it hard?" can be given from the experience of anyone learning in a new field if he is willing to be conscious of his own reactions. Learning on this level is always hard and painful in proportion to the extent to which it involves the self. It can be accomplished only if one is willing to admit the hardness and the fear and put oneself into the task of learning. If there is a teacher, somewhere, somehow, in the process there must be some admission that the teacher knows what the learner does not and a giving-in to this painful, fearful difference which permits an exchange between teacher and pupil. True, superficial learning of subject matter or skills may involve so little of the self that the essential nature of the learning process need never become conscious. But in all professional training the negative elements of the process, the fear, the resistance, and the struggle, can be recognized if one will but look at them.

In all professional education except social work, these reactions are taken for granted as elements to be overcome with as little dwelling upon them as possible. A student entering a medical school is committed to grueling study, to

59

sacrifice, to discipline, if he is to arrive at his goal. He expects to resist it but stakes himself to accomplish it. But social casework, to a greater degree than any other profession, asks its students to become conscious of this conflict within themselves as the very basis for learning how to help others. In this sense alone there is some validity in the accusation that social casework makes training hard, since it requires the student who would deny the hardness and the fear, who tends to handle the new situation in which he finds himself with the superficial, one-sided assertion that he is having no problem, that everything is all right, to break up this assumption in order to gain true understanding of the forces involved in taking help, both for himself and for his client.

The supervisor who accepts responsibility for her function with a student should know from the very beginning of the process that she must help the student to get to some awareness and some expression of these negative aspects of his experience. She must look sharply into the situation, the fieldwork assignment and the supervisory setup, to see what aspects of it may bear harshly upon the student, new to its requirements, or which ones may be used to carry his whole diffused sense of discomfort and awkwardness. It would be wiser to assume that he does not altogether want to be there in that particular fieldwork agency under her supervision than to take for granted that it is exactly what he wanted. She can at least recognize the difficulties of getting to the agency, and for every student these usually loom large. Hopefully, many positive conditions of work will be offered him— his own desk and its equipment as well as clear and accurate information about how to find his way in the agency and the community. A conference hour, defined as to purpose, length, and frequency, for his use surely carries first of all its positive supportive meaning but the supervisor must be alert to recognize its limiting implications as well. It requires the student to organize himself and his material for discussion. He must send in a record of his interviews with the client in advance and present himself on time. Even the limitation of the conference period to one hour, or one hour and a half, has a negative aspect for him. Certainly it limits his freedom to come when he feels like it and to leave in the same way. It may feel too short or too long as it faces him with time that he does not know how to use.

True, these seem but little things, matters to which any student should be expected to adjust with more or less tolerance and a certain amount of healthy criticism of the powers that be. Any student is startled to find himself asked to go below his easy tolerance, to put his criticism out in the open upon a person who holds herself responsible for the conditions that irritate him. He withdraws from the first indication of the supervisor's effort to touch these unacceptable feelings that no one before has ever asked him to face as his own. And since he also feels this expectation in every contact with the School, with teachers as well as supervisor, it begins to constitute a sense of strangeness in the environment, to be felt and resisted as a definite pressure for some response that he has never given before. Students try to understand this in their own discussions with each other and, with the help of the teacher in the casework class, get the courage to articulate their fears of this unknown and dimly sensed demand. Their apprehension may be voiced as an accusation: "You are trying to change us." The answer, "Surely you must change if you are going to learn how to help people but no one can possibly change you against your will and yourself," does not satisfy until they have had more experience with the beginnings of change in themselves. But the experience of discussing their fear and of placing their criticisms directly upon the teacher, who stands for this whole training process and who accept their reactions as natural, helps immeasurably toward a recognition of the validity of these reactions as a part of themselves. But it is with the supervisor in an individual conference hour that the student should have the opportunity to go further in expressing his negative reactions, to learn to place them courageously where they belong.

The supervisor, too, will have more opportunity than the teachers to see the student's negative reactions expressed in behavior as she is closer to his daily contacts with his clients and with other aspects of agency. The best efforts of the most positive, constructive student to conform, to do right, to make good, must break down somewhere in relation to the multitudinous demands that a fieldwork placement in a strange agency puts on him for a new use of himself. Some of his errors are due to ignorance and inexperience and must be understood as such with patient explanation and with encouragement to try again. But other behavior which merits criticism may be due entirely to his resistance to something just because it is asked of him, or even more deeply to the limitations and controls that hem him in. The supervisor must be on the lookout for these manifestations of his unwilling or negative relation to the strange experience of being supervised and face him with it in some specific illustration if she can find it or in general terms when his problem of relating to agency seems more diffuse or more total. She may say: "Your recording has come to me too late for me to read it before conference several times now. I wonder why. Is there anything stenographic service can do about getting it typed or do you think there is something you can do? Perhaps you mind putting down what you have said in an interview in black and white or having me see it to discuss it with you. Could we talk about it?" Or perhaps the student is punctilious about getting his work done and his records typed, but the supervisor is disturbed by a vague sense of unreality in the student's conference discussion, a formality that seemingly accepts, but actually excludes, the supervisor's participation. She may have to take up just this aspect as something in feeling between them with no more to use as illustration than her own feeling that there is something wrong.

It is apparent that what is called for here is more than an external, superficial picking out of something to criticize in the student's work or of something wrong in the fieldwork situation on which the student can express his criticism. This would be easy enough to do and to teach if one had conviction that it was called for. But the more one tries to teach this to a succession of supervisors, the deeper grows one's realization of the forces in human nature that struggle against this responsibility. In spite of the fact that every supervisor has surely learned in a casework process that every client must project upon the worker the negative attitudes aroused by the limitations and conditions of the casework situation if a real and profitable relationship is to develop, she stands back, averse to taking any initiative in helping the student, her client in this training process, to uncover these attitudes in himself in relation to what the training process is demanding of him. Any caseworker finds it more natural to believe in the positive tendency of her own intentions as they bear upon the other person whom she wants to help and to move into a relationship by expressing these and by encouraging the positive attitudes of the other person. Even though she may have come to believe it necessary for the other person to find and face his negative feelings in relationship, she may well feel aversion for the effort it takes to withdraw herself from the flow of a positive movement into the kind of organization of herself and her own forces which is required to meet the other with a new focus that he must recognize and respond to.

More is implied here than the concept of ambivalence now generally accepted in psychiatry and so glibly used in social casework literature. What I am saying is not only that human behavior is characteristically ambivalent but that there is, in spite of every evidence to the contrary, a persistent and fundamental tendency in the natural helper to deny the negative aspect of feeling and to try again and again to build wholes which exclude those negative tendencies. This effort to exclude, to deny, the "bad" in the self, to control and punish its expressions in the self and in others, begins in the earliest relationship with the mother and continues on in the family into school and later relationships. Some individuals succeed in keeping the self all "good" in its intentions toward others and even in its behavior. Perhaps these individuals must make other people good too, are incapable of believing evil of anyone within their environment. Individuals who must have the world they live in wholly good are likely to need a devil to carry the burden of the evil they cannot assimilate. There are those who maintain goodness and rightness in the self only by distributing the evil onto others in the environment; they may tend to be apprehensive and suspicious of others, to blame them rather than to find anything wrong in the self.

True, there are individuals who build up the self aggressively on an affirmation of badness, who want to get the better of the other fellow, even to destroy him. But individuals with this pattern do not often come into training for social work. Those who choose social work as a profession have long since, probably in their earliest relationship, identified the self with goodness, and want to do good to the other. No theoretical teaching about ambivalence touches this fundamental organization of the self, but it must be touched if it is to deal with the reality of human "badness" as it needs to be expressed by the client in the relationship of taking help from an agency. Benevolence must somehow break up its own organization in order to find in the self, and be able to identify with, the evil inherent in all human nature.

This badness can be felt by any individual in a relationship that controls him in any way, as the supervisory relationship necessarily does. He will use his well-established ways of keeping knowledge of his own feelings from himself and, at any cost, from the other person. Any indication of the presence of feeling in himself which he does not want to recognize will be warded off with denial. If this denial is not recognized and accepted, it will tend to break through into consciousness in a sense of confusion and pain. Here is something coming at him from the outside, which must be given some credence by the student since it is accepted as valid in the training process he himself has elected. If he can really see and admit that he has done something wrong in spite of his good intentions, felt critical of the supervisor or the teacher in spite of his belief that everything was good and right in his situation, then actually something new and different has entered into the organization of the self that he brought to training. How deeply a student takes this depends on the nature of the expressed badness, the extent to which he has staked himself, and the amount of the self which is already involved in the training relationship. For young people in the first phase of training, this initial experience may be relatively slight and need not disturb the self very deeply.

While a supervisor may have the deepest conviction theoretically about the nature of the responses the student will feel to the supervisory function, of his fear and resistance to engaging in this new enterprise under the restraints of supervision, if she is inexperienced she often lacks the skill to help the student bring out the feelings he has been taught to hide. Perhaps she can offer only a verbal recognition of the negative feelings whose existence she suspects but cannot bring to a focus. Sometimes even this verbal expression constitutes enough release to enable the process to go on developing until the time when some circumstance precipitates it into a deeper level.

In the following excerpt from a supervisor's record of an early conference with a student, it is interesting to see how relievingly the student can place her fear and resistance on the record and on the supervisor's right to read and criticize it when she is given a little help from the supervisor in expressing her feelings.

Discussion of written material on student's first interview.

We had already discussed this visit briefly and spontaneously when student had come in right afterwards to tell me about it. I had said to her that if she were bursting with it when she came back after this first home visit, she could just call me and if I were free I would be so glad to hear about it. . . . Then last week she had brought me this written material to talk about using it for class purposes. At that time we had talked about how it felt to write and submit this first interview. We had not discussed the recording itself since I had not read it.

I had suggested it had probably been far from easy. She said thoughtfully that it was more difficult than she had foreseen and put it all on the problem of recalling what had happened, and its sequence. I asked lightly if this had been the whole difficulty, and as if searching herself she said, "Yes." I waited a little, and then I asked her if any of the difficulty had to do with me. She looked up at me startled, and then began to bring out how really hard it had been because she had to account for what she had done, and she had kept worrying over whether she had been aware of everything that had happened—whether she had understood it—and what was the proper way to handle it. And then almost whispering, she said, that as she wrote, it had almost become a question of whether to be honest or not. I said yes, it was that hard to reveal oneself. And after a pause I added that it was pretty frightening to see how deeply and even disturbingly involved you get in this learning relationship. We sat on a while thinking, and then I said something I can't recall, that expressed some very genuine confidence I had in her and called for some acknowledgment of at least a measure of confidence in herself that she could find her way in it, probably.

It is interesting to see how for the student this recognition of problem in her own performance begins to strike deep into the area of the bad and fearful in herself. "Almost whispering, she said, that as she wrote, it had almost become a question of whether to be honest or not." The supervisor's response to this is a warm recognition of the student's feeling as her own while at the same time it identifies that feeling as characteristic of this very experience of working with a supervisor and risking the involvement she was beginning to feel in it. One can feel here the beginning of something new in relationship for the student and the support which the supervisor's warm acknowledgment gives to that beginning.

In this period while the supervisor is engaged in trying to help the student express his negative feelings about supervision, classes in the School, particularly the so-called "Personality Course,"[1] either "Attitudes and Behavior," or "The Nature of the Self," challenge and encourage students to risk verbal expression of parts of the self that have been inhibited as impulsive or bad in previous experience. An article by Jessie Taft entitled "Living and Feeling," first printed in *Child Study* in 1933 and mimeographed for the use of students, has been found most valuable as it affords legitimate opportunity for students to focus their negative feeling on a point of view where they can differ and criticize freely. In working on this article in the classroom or in conference with the teacher who stands for the point of view it presents, students typically come to a new and revealing experience and acceptance of negative aspects of themselves.

To call this experience, as is so glibly done by the average caseworker, "releasing the negative" is to misunderstand completely its significance and value in the training movement. On the contrary, it indicates the first stirrings in the self of a spontaneity out of which may develop a freer, more creative use of the self in response to the client's ambivalence and leads to the discovery of hidden and denied forces concealed beneath the conventional and cherished patterns of behavior, potential strengths, without which the wholeness and flexibility essential for the professional use of the self in a helping process can never be achieved.

[1] For a detailed account of the "Personality Course" and its function in the curriculum, see the article entitled "The Function of the Personality Course in the Practice Unit" by Jessie Taft in *Training for Skill in Social Case Work*.

Students who put themselves into this training process most deeply often come through this phase of the revelation of their own negative selves with a positive realization of the value of feeling itself, both positive and negative, so well expressed in Dr. Taft's article in these words:

The price one pays for success in denying negative feelings is a lessening of the ability to feel positively. Feeling is one. It goes with whatever the self admits as vitally important. To be able to feel, one must be willing to care. And to care is to expose one's self to loss or injury or defeat as well as to fulfillment and success. The goodness or badness of an emotion is determined, then, not by pleasantness or unpleasantness, not by its positive or negative, uniting or separating character, but by the extent to which the individual accepts it as a part of himself, a necessary reflection of his own evaluation of living, instead of projecting it completely upon an external cause.[2]

[2] "Living and Feeling." Mimeographed article copied by permission from *Child Study*, January 1933, p. 4.

CHAPTER VII

HELPING THE STUDENT TO FIND A BEGINNING IN HIS CONTACT WITH THE CLIENT

Each time a supervisor launches a new student or a worker new to agency into this enterprise of offering the service of the agency to those who seek its help, she must make vivid and alive for herself again the confusions and the difficulties that this new person encounters. No matter what her experience and skill, she herself must begin again in her own realization of and participation in this process. How can the student enter a client-centered situation already related to agency through countless complicated connections? How follow another worker? Does he study the record and attempt to follow through on what has already been initiated? Can that be done? The supervisor's own problem here is always in taking too much for granted, in not knowing how to get at the questions which every student needs to ask and does not dare to, at what he feels and cannot express.

The student in the interview cited in the previous chapter may be quoted again to give us the lively sense we need of the problems that confronted her, an inexperienced young person, in getting started with a foster mother and an eighteen-months-old boy recently placed in her home. The foster mother is a mature, steady person who has given years of reliable service to the placement agency. She welcomed the student cordially, talking freely about the child, how much the family likes him, etc. She introduced, however, some feeling about the members of the child's family who visit. The student responded on a warm, human level and came out of the interview with some exhilaration. She described her feeling to the supervisor as follows:

Once she left the foster home she felt it had been all right. She

69

had gone out to get acquainted and to give them the chance to get to know her too—they had made a friendly beginning, and that seemed good. Still she knew she had felt stopped, too, by the fear that she might have to do something that would not be entirely friendly.

How clearly this student states for us, what she herself does not as yet know, that the exhilaration she felt immediately after the interview was only the relief of having got through the dreaded visit at all. That it was friendly seems good, but she knows too well that this friendliness was of the foster mother's making and that her own stand has not yet been taken. She suspects and fears that "she might have to do something that would not be entirely friendly." Interestingly, she projects this fear into an unknown future and conceives of herself and the difference she may have to introduce into this good foster-home situation as "unfriendly." This projection of the inevitable fear that grows out of not feeling one's own part in a situation is characteristic. Characteristically, everyone skips the awareness of fear in the present and dodges the realization that hostility is felt in what is immediately going on between two people rather than in the vague "what I might have to do to them in the future."

The supervisor tries to bring the student into this present problem. How difficult it is for her to touch it, how impossible for the student to face it as yet, is evidenced in the recording.

From this we explored whether it might have been helpful to her and Mrs. S. to talk about the change in visitors—to give Mrs. S. a chance to say whether she had been anxious over it—perhaps to say something about the previous worker—maybe to talk over together whether she would be visiting with about the same frequency—that Mrs. S. could feel free to call her at the office too. Student participated by listening thoughtfully, not filling in the gaps of time I left for her own suggestions, but saying she knew what I meant. There was a little questioning how, exactly, she could do it—a little feeling that the recording left out her beginning statement to Mrs. S. that she was the new worker—but she hadn't known how to carry it on, she still couldn't see. I thought perhaps she could use this kind of beginning around her own feelings: "I've been so anxious to meet you, Mrs. S."—and see where that took them.

The student wondered if it were too late to use what she sees now. She really struggled with this and verbalized her thinking. She was sure the questions about her own family would recur. But could she begin with Mrs. S. when the beginning is past? She didn't think she could try saying, "We didn't get to talking much last time about," etc., etc. I agreed the time might be past for it. She wasn't even sure she could bring in some information about how they would be working together as to spacing of visits for the time being, or the fact that she would expect to be the worker till summer.

She returned then to her question, vaguely stated, that she felt she didn't know exactly what things meant as they happened, or how to use herself. She did know her function in representing a child-placing agency. She knew quite certainly her focus was the child but the problem was in living this out piece by piece in her varying day-to-day experiences and relationships. I had to leave her with this. I thought she had the courage to work at it and share it with me. She wasn't sure—somehow she goes ahead in spite of a lack of great courage.

The supervisor ends her record of this conference with her own sense of bafflement for having worked on too much without ever succeeding in making a point clear to the student.

One feels that the supervisor is justified in her belief that this student will go ahead and work on this, but correct, too, in her own sense of failure to give the student help in getting hold of any real sense of herself in this situation. It could have come only if the student had been able to face what it would mean to feel her newness and its meaning to the foster mother. The supervisor, in talking round and about this, succeeds only in blurring all its edges. Evidently the supervisor herself construes the beginning with this foster mother as a purely positive experience when she suggests the student might introduce herself with "I've been so anxious to meet you, Mrs. S." Only if the supervisor herself can face this beginning in all its aspects can she help the student to state her own feelings of fear and inadequacy first and, relieved of them, to give some freedom to look at how it feels to a foster mother to have a new person enter her home. Out of this discussion they should come to a clearer conviction for the student of the immediate purpose of this visit and of the basic agency relationship to this home which can sustain the student and foster mother through the student's new contact.

An older student with several years of successful experience in a child-placing agency before she entered training reveals the same problem in beginning in a new fieldwork placement, the problem of trying to find a role for herself as counselor in a public school. In contrast to the younger student's feeling of vague, undefined fear, she is full of impatience and irritation, baffled by her ignorance and inability to act, in contrast with the sureness she had felt in her child-placing experience. Her vigor and determination to find a way forces the supervisor to struggle with her on the problem she brings to this conference at the beginning of the fieldwork placement. The interview she wants to discuss is her first interview with a boy referred as a health problem by a teacher. She feels only dissatisfaction with what she has done, confusion as to what she could do.

I quote the conference as the supervisor recorded it:

I wondered then whether she felt that there was a problem in this case. "Oh, yes, she did," she said. There was no question in her mind that the boy's health was causing trouble, or would cause a problem in the future in his relation to the school. I asked whether she felt that as a counselor, she had a function here. She was sure that she did, implying that I wouldn't have assigned the case to her otherwise, but she added honestly that she didn't know what to do. She knew that there were problems in all the cases I gave her, and she thought she knew the treatment they needed, but she just didn't know how to go about handling them. "What do you say to a child, when you send for him, to make him respond?"

I recognized warmly that it is awfully hard to know just how to begin with a child, and frightening, too, particularly when you have to initiate the contact and it is someone other than he who asks help for him. Perhaps we could begin to find some answer to these questions, if we examined the interview bit by bit.

We began this carefully with my questioning her elaborate explanation to the teacher of her role as counselor. She followed for a few minutes, then suddenly interrupting me, she burst out that she was feeling so clumsy and awkward in handling interviews. She thought she knew something about casework before she came here; now she was feeling that she knew nothing, as if she had never talked to a child. She couldn't get hold of anything with him; she didn't know what she was doing, really. And then, not knowing resources in the school, or its regulations and standards, she could never be sure whether she was doing the right thing.

I said that, of course, she couldn't know, and certainly she would be bound to make mistakes. Anyone coming into a large institution like this would feel confused and helpless until she could acquire a little more facility in using the mechanics. But, also, her relationship here was quite different than it had been in a placement agency, wasn't it? She said yes. Here one is concerned only with school adjustment; in child placing one is concerned with the total life of a child. Here she knows nothing about the background in the home or the family before talking with a child. I recognized that this could make her feel pretty insecure, and added that she felt less needed here, too, didn't she? Yes, that bother her, although, she added quickly, she knew that a counselor must be needed here.

I said warmly that I thought I knew something of what she must be going through, and that this beginning as a student wasn't easy for her. It seemed to me, although perhaps it didn't to her just now, that her experience in working with children in another agency was not entirely useless, and that she was bringing something to this new experience. However, only as she acquired more experience in working on individual cases, and began using resources outside and within herself, could she begin to feel more comfortable. And through this, I'd be going right along with her, and trying to help her as much as I could.

Student sat back, still looking disturbed. I waited quietly for a moment or two, but she seemed to have nothing more to say, and so I went back to the case material.

I wondered whether she had any question about the way in which she had presented to Philip her understanding of his problem. She said she didn't think so. We talked then a little about the feeling of this boy, who, she recognized with me, was probably pretty frightened at being summoned to see this strange person in the school who seemed to know so much about him. Student could go along with me on this, but she looked puzzled when I stopped. I asked then if she thought she might have been able, at this point, to relate herself a little more to the school in the boy's mind, and at the same time give him a little more security by bringing in his teacher's part in the situation. She agreed but it was obvious that she herself was not feeling related to the question. I pressed her further by asking why she had thought it best *not* to tell Philip who had made the referral?

Her face cleared, and she smiled. "Of course," she said, "I should have told him that the teacher had told me about him." We discussed then the advantages of such an approach, in terms of her own relationship with the boy. It seemed to me that she had really found a point of entrance for herself into this situation at last.

The difference between this conference and the first lies, not only in the greater capacity of this experienced student to take hold of the concrete aspects of the boy's problem and her determination to seek for her own effective role in it, but also in the supervisor's keener awareness of the painful nature of the feelings aroused in the student by being caught in a situation where she does not know where to turn. She is more able to stay with this problem, to help the student verbalize it and bring out all the factors in it. Evidently, the most difficult factor in this situation for the student is the relationship of the boy's teacher who makes the referral. It asks her to find for herself a different and more partial responsibility for the boy to whom she will act as counselor than for the child whom she would place in a foster home. How firmly the supervisor holds her to facing this precise point when she asks, "Why had she thought it best *not* to tell Philip who had made the referral?" The student's relief at this is obvious. The barrier between herself and the teacher, between herself and the boy, is down as she can take in the supervisor's question. One sees that she is ready to make a realistic beginning with Philip as she is now identified with her function as school counselor.

Finally, I should like to look at this problem of beginning from the record of an experienced supervisor working with an experienced student. This student is in her thirties and brought to training some years of work as a visitor in a public agency and in Red Cross Home Service. She had taken extension courses in the School before entering training. In spite of the fact that she was coming to school on her own initiative and with a purpose which she had long had in mind, she approached the actual experience very negatively and had much to fight out, first in the admissions process and then with her teachers, before she could get herself into the situation at all. To the fieldwork placement, a coveted opportunity in the neuropsychiatric service of a large military hospital and her own first choice of placement, she brought her most positive efforts to learn what was there to be learned.

There is much to be mastered in the orientation to the external physical aspects of a large military hospital. Just to find one's way around constitutes a major problem. Beneath these spatial connections lie the much more complicated network of relationships of military, medical, and psychiatric authorities and the delicate thread of responsibility for the individual patient carried by the social worker, in this situation representing the Red Cross. The most skillful caseworker would be hesitant in finding her way into this situation. This student whose experience I quote is not skillful, but vigorous, powerful, quick to action, determined to learn. The following conference, which describes her effort to make a beginning with Private X, a plastic surgery patient, took place in the middle of November after six weeks of training.

The supervisor states her impression of the student's learning problem, her pressure on the supervisor to give her rule, policy, and procedure, in the following introduction to the conference.

Student from the beginning spoke about *skill* repeatedly. It was what she wanted to learn. It was what she came to school and to X General Hospital "to get." At the same time she pressed me to tell her "what your policy is" or "what is the practice of the Military." I was much troubled by these questions, at a loss to know how to handle them. It seemed strange to me to speak in such grandiose terms of "the practice of the Military" in relation to such a simple thing as telephoning a medical officer to ask him whether it would be convenient to refer a patient to him for approval of a loan application.

The supervisor's record goes on to relate the discussion of the case of Private X. I quote it in full.

I had picked up the case of Private X among several others student had given me for routine reading. He was a patient on a plastic surgery ward and during May had made a loan of $15 for the purpose of financing an unexpected furlough home. He had agreed at that time to repay the loan on June 20. This had not been done. Student had seen the patient on 10-26 in reference to a matter concerning a brother, also in the service, who had requested an extension of his furlough in order that he and the patient might have more time to spend together. I should not fail to mention that the previous worker on the case, who was the same worker who had made the loan in May to the patient, had seen the patient on 10-25, just one day before student had visited him. On neither visit was the matter of the delinquent loan mentioned. I was curious about student's failure to pick this up.

During our conference on November 12 I discussed this case with her. I opened the discussion by asking her whether she had been aware that there was an unpaid loan in this case of Private X when she had visited him. She looked troubled and agreed that she had been aware of this but did not know what "one did in cases like this."

I wondered what she thought should be done. She pondered on this in silence. Finally and cautiously she ventured that as a caseworker she thought the matter of the unpaid loan should be discussed with Private X but "as a Red Cross caseworker I don't know what should be done." She was puzzled by the fact that the previous worker had not mentioned it and did not know what her own obligation was and also by the knowledge that her own earlier experience in a Red Cross setup had not given her a basis for procedure here.

I suggested that we might try to consider why it was important to pick up this matter of the unpaid loan, from the point of view of agency and from the point of view of the patient.

We discussed these two points fully, and at our conclusions student nodded solemnly. When I thought we were finished with the discussion of this case and looked down at the material on my desk to pick up the next case I wanted to give her, meanwhile handing the X case record to her, I was genuinely startled, when I heard her exclaim, "Oh, no, I'm not finished with it yet!"

I agreed to continue the discussion by asking her what more she would like to ask about the X case. There was a silence and then, "This takes skill. Where do you get it?"

This was said with such a spontaneous gesture of helplessness on her part, so different from her usual ability to raise logical questions that I laughed and said, "But you don't 'get' it, do you?" "Of course," was her immediate response, and then she went on to describe rather pedantically her concept of the acquirement of skill. I did not agree with this concept but did not express my disagreement at this time because it did not seem important.

What did seem important to me was to know whether student was afraid of getting into this situation of the loan. There was an emphatic denial, followed by a wordy dissertation on the cause of her hesitancy. I really could not follow what she was saying—

it was so devious and complicated and I asked her if she would repeat it. She tried to but after a few words floundered helplessly.

I ventured that what she had really said, I thought, was that she was afraid, wasn't it? She nodded her head. We discussed further the reasons for this, her sense of discomfort about going to see a patient about a loan and her feeling of "dunning." We reviewed what seemed "right" for us to do here, "right" for the patient and "right" for the agency. When she seemed ready to leave the X case, I suggested that she might not be able to do this thing we had decided was "right." If she could not do it, I wanted her to know that we could discuss it again before she visited Private X on his ward. This appeared to finish the question satisfactorily for her that day and it was on this note that we left the case of Private X.

This conference contains the essential elements of what must be faced and struggled through between supervisor and student and student and client in making a real beginning in a process of learning to help through casework function. It is instructive to see the value which the actual negative element in the situation, the unpaid loan, contributes. Here was something between student and client which could not be skipped, something which her own sound feeling told her was troubling her and must trouble the patient. The fact that she herself was not responsible for making the loan seems an almost insuperable problem in finding her relation to him on it, but at the same time it introduces Red Cross into the situation as the consistent, responsible agent to which both she and the patient are obligated. Only when she can really admit her fear of facing the patient with his obligation, and of the personal feeling of dunning that overwhelms her, can she get beyond this to look at what is "right" for patient and for agency.

It is interesting to see that it is the student's sense of problem, her determination to see this through to something basic, that holds the supervisor in the beginning of this discussion. The supervisor had finished with the case and handed it back when the student refused to leave it. But how immediate is the supervisor's response to this indication of the student's need! From this point on she takes the lead to get beneath the student's verbalizations about skill to the simple admission that she is afraid to face the patient with a question about the loan. She realizes that this discussion may not settle it for the student and tells her she can discuss it again, if necessary, before she sees the patient.

One senses that the student leaves this conference with something basically focused between herself and the supervisor so clearly and definitely that it will inevitably move to some new resolution. The student brings this eagerly to the next conference.

The following Monday, November 19, student gave me the case of Private X to read for our next conference. Her face fairly glowed with excitement as she gave me the case, saying smilingly, "I tried what you said and it worked!" I must admit to being startled. I could not recall that I had given her any formula and I wondered what it was she meant.

I learned that she still had a great deal of feeling about seeing Private X, saying that it would have seemed more comfortable to her "if I had been in on the ground floor," meaning if she had been the worker who had made the loan. This was followed by a wistful statement that she supposed that this "could never happen in Red Cross, though." I thought that was not really so and I asked her to examine this critically. She could not do this, it seemed, so I brought to her attention how even in a child-placing agency, which to her was an agency that seemed to represent the quintessence of all that was professional, a worker frequently had to go into the middle of a situation created or begun by another worker.

I continued by asking her to tell me what it was she did when she so directly focused on the purpose of her interview on 11-19 with Private X. She fairly glowed as she said excitedly that she "had cut through to get to the point." We discussed this further with my directing the discussion to the end of helping her see why this visit of hers for this purpose was acceptable to the patient, although it was not *she* who had made the loan.

She was very thoughtful as I pointed this up by saying that for the first time in her experience here she had projected herself as "Miss M., a Red Cross caseworker." It was she who crystallized this still further by commenting with excitement, "I see it now. That's why I had the *right* to go to see Private X about the loan."

We were able to go on from here to discuss what had been unreal in her previous, intense striving for skill as separated from function and—it was she who said it—that skill had to be related to function and that function was the purpose of your agency, of which the caseworker was representative. She could understand why Private X could accept her, because although she was new to him, the Red Cross was not new to him. It was the agency with which he had dealt in May when he had made the loan.

What has taken place in these two conferences on Private X? A complete shake-up in the student's identifications and attitudes toward casework which she brought to school in the first place and had been holding to tightly and determinedly. These attitudes maintained an effective barrier between herself, the untrained Red Cross Home Service worker, and the trained supervisor who knows how and should be able to give her the rule for proceeding in every contact. Her feelings of hostility against all those who know how when she does not, have been persistently pounding against this barrier. They had been released to some extent in a previous conference with her adviser. In consequence of this, she brings to this conference with her supervisor on Private X a kind of readiness to move out of this negative phase of relationship. With the supervisor's help, all her feelings become focused around the unpaid loan and she is able to admit fear of her own negative feelings as well as of the other person's negative. Actually, this amounts to realization of the fear of facing the other person with responsibility for her own feeling and action. To take the next step, then, is to move into the beginning of the professional helping relationship. In doing it, the student leaves behind the old Red Cross self and identifies herself with a new Red Cross self, exemplified in the supervisor. She is triumphant in her conviction about what she was able to do with Private X in the interview about the loan and can put into vivid words her understanding of what she had done: "she had cut through to get to the point." No words could describe better what the supervisor had done with her in the previous conference. As soon as this new identification is felt and used with the client, the student gets a completely different understanding of function. It comes with a sense of revelation that now she has a right to see the patient about the loan and that it is this conviction of hers that enables him to accept it.

These two experiences just quoted, that of the student in the school-counseling placement and the student in the military hospital, epitomize the beginning phase of the training experience. It is typical of the movement that must take place through the projection of negative attitudes and on to a new positive identification with the supervisor which enables a real identification with the function of the agency to be established. The one student can talk with the boy comfortably when she is free to identify herself with the counseling function of the supervisor and to recognize the teacher's role, not as one that threatens her, but as related to her own, yet different. She can use the teacher's referral now to make her contact with the boy, instead of feeling cut off from him by it. The other student as she identifies with her supervisor finds her right, as Red Cross worker in a military hospital, to talk to the patient about the loan.

This beginning phase of the training movement has come to the desired eventuation in six weeks in these two placements and should in every situation not be delayed longer than eight weeks. If the supervisor is not alert enough to recognize and focus the confusion for the student, there will be an increase of fear, a mounting of negative feeling, a pressure on the supervisor, which will ultimately explode in some way. Out of such an explosion, a realistic beginning can often be retrieved if the supervisor has integrity and willingness to see what she has done and the strength to make an honest admission of fault without giving up her function as supervisor.

Through all the various details of case situations and the differences in functions, in skill and experience of supervisors and students analyzed in this chapter, one fundamental and important point for an understanding of the activity of the supervisor in this training process stands out clearly. It can be generalized in these words: only when the supervisor finds a way to cut through the case detail and take hold of the student himself courageously, to focus on something immediately present in the student's feeling or attitude in the situation or toward herself, can the student get hold of a direct and responsible connection with his client. The new feeling which emerges for the student out of this experience first with his supervisor, then with his client, constitutes his earliest beginning experience of a focus in his use of himself and the responsible connection it creates between oneself and the other. Out of this experience can come a true conviction of the meaning and use of function.

CHAPTER VIII

THE TURNING POINT IN THE PROCESS

The learning movement which has come through the beginning phase in the training process now moves into an extended plateau on which the student is typically occupied with using this newly acquired sense of function throughout his case load. There seems to be a brief respite from struggle, a sense of effectiveness and achievement. There is consciousness of a new strength which comes from identification with the supervisor and the agency. The casework class, into which are brought illustrations of the beginning experiences of different students learning to represent their different functions, carries further the conviction of the meaning of this training experience and establishes the beginning of a new relationship in the group—a relationship based on professional experience, not personal liking or disliking.

The supervisor may find great reward and satisfaction in this period in the revelations the student brings back to her, in his positive sense of exploration and learning. However, there need be no fear that the student will rest content on this plateau if the supervisor is free enough to trust the dynamics of the casework relationships themselves and the student's own movement in them and in his relationship to the supervisor to call out new responses in the student. If she keeps her sensitivity to the student and watches for indications of his confusions and blockings, she should know when and what to tackle with him in conference discussion and how to hold him to working through his next area of conflict. On the other hand, no supervisor, least of all one without experience and skill in this process, finds it easy to break up a peaceful interval by holding the student to a fresh realization of problem in order to engage him in a new and deeper learning struggle. The beginning engagement may seem to be enough, the positive gains as she sees them in the student's casework may appear sufficiently satisfactory to justify her in continuing the easy way of going along at the student's pace.

One may well ask: "What is there, then, to set the pace other than the speed of an intelligent and willing student?" No school of social work, to my knowledge, has ever succeeded in setting up criteria for what should be learned in a first month or a second, in a first or a second semester. Many have been intrigued by this possibility but have fallen down in the task with some realization, perhaps, that the helping process we seek to teach is not of a nature to lend itself to the one, two, three pattern of standardized, objectified learning goals. But the fact remains that there is a helping process to be learned, a process whose rhythm and speed of movement take place in a time form set up by the school. In the process I am describing here, the pattern of the fifteen-week semester, the two-semester year, and the two-year graduate program has been in use for many years. I believe that it does not matter what this time form is so long as it is understood and used by the school as the unit within which movement takes place. The mere fact of the acceptance of a unit of time within which something is to take place gives to both participants in the process a certain relation to the time limits of that movement within each hour and as a whole. Each moves with it or against it, controls it or yields to it, fills the hour with content or leaves it empty and barren, because of the deep underlying necessity of each human being to move in relationship from a beginning to an end. The pressure to finish, to accomplish within the time limit, at the same time the fear of ending and of not being ready to end, operate in every task and in every time-limited relationship. Inevitably these fears and pressures operate for both student and supervisor in the training process. To deny them only increases their potency. If they can be admitted and recognized they can be utilized for the student's learning, a learning that he recognizes first as his own experience but one that is immediately translatable into his relations with his client.

Only the structures and convictions of the professional school evolved out of long experience can offer sufficient support to enable the supervisor herself to be free to move and to help her student to move forward within the training structure of the time-limited term or semester. If she listens carefully to her student she will find in the very earliest conferences some question, some scarcely articulated fear, about "evaluation." "How will I know if I am doing well, or enough?" The plateau I have been describing, which follows the student's identification with agency function somewhere between the sixth and eighth week of training, will finally be invaded by some question which refers to evaluation and which is an indication that the student is looking ahead in time, if only apprehensively. The teacher regards this sixth to eighth week period as a mid-semester point when she herself, in her own thinking, is tentatively evaluating her students, returning papers to them with some significant comment or question. The students react to this with an increase of fear and questioning, with discussion among themselves and often class discussion that articulates and focuses the fear of movement on "Am I doing well and enough in class and in the field?" And on a second question, "How will I know how I am doing?"

To show how the supervisor can make use of this questioning on the student's part and help him to find his own role by focusing the problem specifically in the casework and supervisory process, I have selected two conferences occurring in the seventh and eighth weeks of training between a supervisor and a student placed in an agency offering a service to the families of boys committed to a reformatory. This student is past his middle twenties, an intelligent, able young man who moves into a new experience positively and eagerly. He is accustomed to doing well whatever he undertakes. He fulfills all assignments on time and with fine consideration for all the factors involved. He has made a good beginning in his fieldwork placement and is one of the first students in his section to offer case material from his own experience for class discussion. The supervisor is a man, a skilled case-worker, new to student supervision.

This material was selected and discussed fully in conference with his supervisor. When the class presentation had taken place, the supervisor told the student he would be making an appointment to talk with the class teacher, the student's adviser, about his work. Such a conference between adviser and supervisor is typical procedure at this time in the semester and it is typical procedure for the student to be told that it will take place.[1] Obviously this focuses fear on what takes place between adviser and supervisor which concerns the student so intimately. He must be helped to find his right relation to the actuality of such a conference through discussing it with supervisor, adviser, or both. Both will want to make some reference to it in order that it may be included in the relationship each has with the student.

The excerpt from the supervisor's record which follows shows the clarification and conviction the supervisor himself has gained from discussing the student's work with the school adviser as both were close to it and saw it projected in the case he had presented in class. This clarification has illuminated his whole point of view of the student's work. While he still feels warmly about the student's ability and good progress, he is able to cut through to a deeper focus of problem and face the student with it.

November 16. We talked of my recent conference with his school adviser for the greater part of the hour. Student had been intensely interested in knowing how the adviser and I felt about him and I had told him that for my part, I felt he was making

[1] For a full discussion of the relation between the adviser and the supervisor, see article by Goldie Basch Faith, entitled "Classroom and Field Work: Their Joint Contribution to Skill," in *Training for Skill in Social Case Work*.

pretty good progress so far. I pointed out evidence of what I meant—his industry, his eagerness, his responsibility and conscientiousness, etc. I had felt that there had been a bit of anxiety on his part up to then and what I said was designed to reassure him. There was no mistaking the comfort and relief he felt. But he wondered how the adviser felt. This, I told him, was something he would have to get from her. I thought that in the main she agreed with me that he was moving along pretty well, but I certainly couldn't speak for her in the details of his progress at school. Student said he would see her next week. Previously he had rationalized his procrastination in making an appointment first by "waiting until a paper was returned" and then "until after I had seen her." I recognized the naturalness of putting off such a meeting when one feels so uncertain about oneself and one's work. He rationalized this again by saying he had delayed until after I had talked with his adviser. "Maybe so," I said, "but I guess you are a bit afraid to go too." This he admitted, but he said he felt better about it in the light of our conference today.

We then directed our attention to some recorded material. This material, an interview with the mother of a boy in X Reformatory, reflected a trend similar to that in the case he had presented in class in the way student is handling cases and learning casework. I told him I sensed a note of urgency on his part to get things done, to put himself into the center of the interview, to get things settled without much regard for the client's need or pace in taking help. I pointed out specific spots in which he "said," "asked," "recommended," "acted," "directed." He dominated the interview almost to the exclusion of the client and her needs at that time. Student nodded and said he was in the picture a lot, wasn't he. I told him I thought it was important to be in the picture but equally important is how you get in and how much of the picture you have to be in so as to satisfy your own needs. Perhaps he would want to consider the pressure he puts on a client and the urgency he feels to get things done. I concluded the conference deliberately at this point saying he might want to think it over.

The supervisor's good judgment in leaving his question with the student at this point for him to think over is confirmed by what the student brings back to the next conference. The day after the conference described he submitted an "agenda" for the next conference listing for consideration at the end:

On my impatience and haste during interviews—my problem as I see it. If possible I would like this definitely on the agenda, even if it entails omitting or reducing the above points.

The record of the conference follows:

November 20. In accordance with student's agenda we started on his problem as he sees it. At the start he said he had thought a lot about what I had said and he guessed it was pretty important. He guessed it was the way he was with people before he ever came here. I thought it likely that impatience to get things done was not something newly acquired but asked him to explain. He went into considerable detail in describing personal relations: he argued a lot with friends and got impatient when they didn't go straight to the point. He cut them off and settled the matter his own way. He got annoyed with fuzzy arguments, disliked "lack of logic." I understood his reactions—they were the core of the academic and intellectual life which he loved and had not yet really left. I said as much. He nodded in agreement. I went on to say that such an approach could hurt a client. For example, he had "logically" and forthrightly tackled with the mother of the boy in X Reformatory the problem raised by his getting a girl in the family way. Student had proceeded step by step in his way, not hers, to the conclusion—that the court would see to it that the boy paid support. "She seemed stunned"—and student left her that way. I pointed this out. Student said grimly that was bad. I agreed, and went on to say there was something good in this, too. His job is to point out what in reality she and her son would have to face; but it is also to recognize the difficulties this would involve for them and to help her with her feelings of fear. He said he guessed he hadn't helped. I didn't spare him; and then pointed out that just as in the case he presented in class, he had gone ahead at *his* speed, conducting the interview toward an end *he* selected, and doing these things without much regard for his client's feelings or need.

Student seemed to expect my reaction because in the agenda

he had contrasted this interview with one in which he quite tenderly helped a weepy father of a reformatory boy understand the industrial school program. I recognized this difference in his work. He explained it in terms of finding a weepy man easier to reach than a reticent woman. When I suggested they might both be afraid of him and reacting differently to this fear, he could see this. He could also see that *he* was different in both interviews and that his problem aggravated the problem of the inaccessible mother because he couldn't adjust himself somewhat to her speed, her fears, her need for healing.

This experience in the middle of the semester constituted a turning point in the student's training movement. This phase of his training grows out of his own active, positive, well-organized self, his readiness to present his own work in class. But it requires his adviser's critical relation to that case and the coming-together of adviser and supervisor in discussion of the student's relation to the case, to enable the student to get beneath his own natural approach to a new use of himself. This evaluative activity also focuses the supervisor's attitude and gives him the conviction to go back to the student with a criticism which can penetrate the student's good adjustment in order to get at the problem his very clarity and logic create for the parent whose feelings they override. While doing this, the supervisor expresses his sincere and spontaneous appreciation of the student's good qualities, as well as sympathetic understanding of his fear of criticism, of evaluation—fear which the student rationalizes and denies to the same extent and in the same way that he overrides the client's fear.

This is not an easy conference for either supervisor or student. Both are involved in it, stirred by it. Left with his own feelings and the supervisor's questions, the student reacts vigorously, carries the questions further, applies them to other cases. There is defense of himself in this but at the same time a new openness to the feelings of the other person as he achieves a freer relation to his own feelings. Between the supervisor and student now there is a realization in more fundamental terms of the student's problem in learning to help a client. One can see that a deeper level of the student's personality has been touched. He refers to all his personal relations with people and is aware of his greater freedom in responding to a father in trouble than to a mother. Obviously this is but the beginning of a movement which will involve his feelings of himself as a man in personal relationships as well as in the helping relationship. But how wisely the supervisor, without cutting off the feeling, keeps it focused around the meaning of his functioning as a person who represents the agency to these troubled clients. Both the mother and the father might be afraid of him and both need something from him, he says. This is a new idea to the student. It pulls together the feelings that have been so personally stirred in himself into something tangible which he can use and move on in learning how to help. One can know that he will ultimately have to go deeper into an exploration and reorganization of these attitudes before he is in full possession of his strength and capacity to help women as well as men clients, but one can feel sure through the record of these two conferences that what he has done at this point is sound and sufficient for the ongoing of the training movement. The supervisor comments on the difference in the student's relation to conference after this experience. He brings his feelings more freely, asks more penetrating questions, and offers his own criticisms of his interviews.

I repeat in concluding this discussion of these two critical conferences that this supervisor was new to student supervision. He was a skilled caseworker, with limited experience in supervising workers. He is honest, frank, direct, and able to use the other parts of the student's school experience to precipitate and sustain the student's movement. His own relation to the school process and the adviser enables him to find the right timing for his action and to trust it to eventuate in the total movement, in spite of the fact that he himself has not experienced this movement through to an ending.

When the School carries full responsibility for the total time structure of the training process and the relation of the parts of this process to the whole, it is justified in using inexperienced supervisors who are willing to lend themselves to this process in all of its newness and through this experience learn its direction and its controls. In doing this, the School can never afford to lose sight of the fact that these inexperienced supervisors are themselves in a process with the School and must be prepared to have them, like the student, resist whatever carries them beyond their own moorings in casework experience. No step, I believe, carries the supervisor further beyond her own known experience and involves greater risk of her professional competence than the necessity of finding a focus, a turning point, in the student's training movement. However stubbornly this step is resisted, it can be accepted, experience proves, through the use of the arbitrary time structures which the School maintains. When the supervisor has worked through this process once with the help of the School, through a turning point to an ending, she will have experienced in herself the feeling of the training movement in a time structure which will enable her to enter into the process with her next student with greater ability to appreciate the necessity for focus and to anticipate the timing of the turning point.

CHAPTER IX

EVALUATION AT THE END OF FIRST SEMESTER

When a turning point has been felt and focused in any relationship process, every person involved begins to have some awareness of the impending end toward which the process inevitably moves. How personal and individual are the reactions to this movement taking place deeply in the organic self, rarely recognized as belonging to the self if indeed they are consciously felt at all, only those who work with this process can understand. What is happening is a shift in equilibrium, a change in direction, a return of the energy which has been so stirred and absorbed by the dynamics of the relationship into its sources in the self. The recipient in the relationship has overcome his initial fear in the beginning phase, has risked some part of himself, has taken in something different from the other person, and now must move away on this newly acquired strength out of the influence and control of the helping person.

This inevitable natural movement to a premature separation and independence is completely obscured by conflicting natural tendencies, by a deeper need for relationship, and by the fear of ending and of independence. In the professional helping relationship, while the tendency to separate must be recognized, the need to remain must be supported in order to enable the individual to stay in the relationship and trust to its deeper movement toward an ending less premature than his first impulsive reaction might dictate.

For the student, the recipient in the supervisory relationship, in order that he may have the experience which will discipline his own tendency so that he can help the client in a similar process, it is obviously necessary that he stay in the relationship. He himself has no question about this necessity, for he accepts intellectually the semester time structure of the school and uses it, not only intellectually, but more deeply to struggle through his natural ambivalence. All the natural fear of ending can be mobilized here and focused on the approaching evaluation which marks the end of the semester's work and is a punctuation mark, if not an ending, in the relationship with the supervisor.[1]

Evaluation takes on more fearful aspects for the student body than the familiar examination process of the college for the reason that the self has been more deeply engaged and more is felt to be at stake in the training movement than in academic learning. As students project and exaggerate this fear in discussion among themselves, there is a natural desire on the part of teachers and supervisors to reduce it by explanation. The most that can be done is by understanding, not denying the fear. Teachers must be alert to the way in which fear is fanned in the whole student body by anything that happens to a single student. The withdrawal of a student before the end of the semester, for instance, may mobilize the fear of all the class around the questions: "Was he asked to leave," and "Will this happen to me?" While premature explanations cannot allay this fear, every opportunity should be offered the student, either individually or in class, to bring out his fear and his questions. As the student can begin to take hold of ending and gets some conception of evaluation as a process in which he himself, as well as the supervisor and adviser, will be active in reviewing his work, fear will yield in some degree to constructive, eager interest and activity.

A definite time structure must be set up for this ending phase of the semester which culminates in the evaluative process, a time structure which must regard and engage teachers, adviser, supervisor, and student in their rightful roles. This timing can be focused on the typed form provided for the evaluation. This form can be distributed to the

[1] In the setup I am describing, students remain in the same placement with the same supervisor for a year.

students in the casework class, at the time it is given to the supervisors in the supervisors' class or to other supervisors by mail. A date must be set by each supervisor for the evaluation conference well in advance to allow the student time for preparation. A later date is set by the School for the return of the completed evaluation to the adviser. The student, through this active relation to the content of the evaluation form, from class discussion which gives him ample opportunity to express his fears about it and at the same time to extend his own actual knowledge of what the evaluation is about, brings to the evaluative conference with his supervisor some ability to participate. He will have thought about the questions the form raises: his case load, his relations to his clients, how he takes help in supervision, his capacity to organize his work, to meet requirements of dictation and of agency schedules, etc. In this process there is an objectification of his work as such, a separation of the work from the self, which in itself constitutes the separation that prepares for and makes bearable the separating, evaluative attitude of the supervisor.

This description may have the effect of making the evaluation process and the evaluation conference between the supervisor and the student appear simple and easy in contrast to the strain of a written evaluation. It is never that for these two individuals who have been actually engaged in a vital learning process, since it necessitates a marked change in the relationship, a standing apart from each other to look at the semester's experience and its accomplishment as a whole. The beginning supervisor finds this detachment difficult to achieve and must be helped to reach it by the emphasis of the School and the adviser on the form and the date-setting for the evaluation conference and for the completed evaluation to be sent to the School. The supervisor-in-training will need to discuss it in class and with the student's adviser just as the student does. She will need to prepare for it by going over the student's work as a whole in her mind and by careful record reading.

If both supervisor and student have prepared for the conference in this way and bring to the actual evaluation conference the readiness to share their findings, there will be no lack of significant content for discussion. There is always some problem, however, when each participant is so well prepared through differentiation and separation and has organized himself and his material so well, in getting together again for participation in a process. The supervisor usually swings between two extremes: taking too much initiative and authority in her effort to establish the fact that this is evaluation, or, in her fear of doing that, leaving the student alone without sufficient support from her. The student, too, who in this experience of being evaluated is brought up sharply against all his fears of authority and criticism, struggles deeply with his fundamental need to control the relationship.

The test of a helpful, satisfactory evaluation conference lies in the feeling of each participant that both have had an effective part in it and that what has been said about the student's work and what will go to the school in the written form are acceptable to both. If the supervisor has expressed her difference and handled her criticisms of the student's work frankly throughout the semester as occasion arose, if she has focused her criticism in terms of a fundamental turning point as described in the preceding chapter, there will be no need to introduce new criticism in this final evaluation conference. Rather it should be the student who takes possession of the criticism now, sees his beginning work in terms of the change he has experienced with its indication of the need for new skill not yet achieved, but which he begins to perceive and reach out for. For the student who is able to do this, there is tremendous satisfaction in this evaluation experience.

Following this evaluation conference, it remains for the supervisor to write out the completed evaluation on the school form. There is much difference of opinion as to whether the final written evaluation should be read by the student. My own experience leads me to believe that if the student has really participated in the conference he will trust the supervisor to submit the evaluation. If asked he will say, "I don't want to read it." Any lack of trust in the supervisor which leads him to fear that she will write something to the School that she has not already said to him implies a fundamental problem in the supervisory relationship which bodes ill for genuine learning. While students, many of them, bring distrust to the beginning of this experience, it should have been worked through by the end of the semester so that the student knows that his supervisor shares with him as well as with the adviser her opinion of his work. Difficult as this three-cornered relationship is for students to understand and accept, they come to do so to a great extent in the first semester, so that reliance and trust in it become stronger than fear and suspicion.

It is argued that there is no reason why the student should not read the evaluation since he knows what goes into it. Anyone who has had the experience of reading his own evaluation knows that a reaction to the finality of the written word produces a very different response from the fluid discussion of that same content. Process goes out of the written word and it becomes endowed with a definiteness and finality that one cannot bear to have placed on one's changing experience. Nor should a changing learning experience ever be asked to carry such definiteness and finality. The supervisor's written record of the student's development belongs in the School, where it plays its part in the total record of his training which constitutes the material out of which the School can draw its final evaluations, recommendations, and references.

The letdown or slump which follows the achievement of any goal in a learning or creative process is a common phenomenon well known to all teachers. Energy has been put out and used up in achieving that goal; the examination or evaluation marks a successful achievement, the finish. Certainly it does not mean the complete exhaustion of energy, but often the release of the new energy unused in the effort to achieve the goal. This fresh energy may dissipate itself in a variety of activities, or it may seek an impulsive expression denied by the obligation to hold itself to one end, or may quickly engage itself in pursuit of a new self-willed goal. All educational institutions understand this phenomenon and handle it in various ways. Usually a brief vacation period follows midyear examinations, a period in which the student can rest, have a good time, free himself from first-semester connections, and get ready to start again. He goes over his equipment, his clothes, his books, and his papers; he registers for the new semester, perhaps choosing new courses, setting up a different schedule. These activities all have their value as signs and symbols of another beginning which will carry him further into his total learning undertaking.

All the phenomena which characterize the output of energy and the renewal of its sources in any learning experience are present to a greater degree in learning to use oneself in a helping process. Constant consideration must be given by those who set up the structures for this training process to the necessity of providing time and opportunity for this shift in energy. That it has not received the consideration it deserves is due, I believe, to the fact that this training process in social work is being developed out of the helping process in social casework, and its timing is still involved with the timing of the casework process in the rendering of the agency's service. There is a fundamental problem here which requires special treatment. For purposes of this discussion, it is important only to see the extent to which students at the time of this midyear shift are already involved in responsibility for service to clients, for carrying a case load however small it may be. It is essential for the student to learn that while his own tendency to slump, to end, to move out of responsibility and relationship must be felt and recognized, he is in this agency and this profession to give to his clients the steady support of the service to which they are entitled.

The supervisor who, in her own training and agency experience, has accepted this discipline of her own impulsive movement will be able to help the student to achieve the same discipline. The necessity arises early, particularly with young students who have not been prepared by anything in college education for the kind of responsibility for clients which professional training asks them to take. Week-ends and Thanksgiving, Christmas, and midyear vacations have been their own time in a way which must be modified in the professional school. For every student, the supervisor's consideration with him of what will be going on in each of his cases during his vacation, or in absence for any cause from agency, is most important in developing in the student the professional responsibility he must learn to carry for his client. It is this deepening sense of responsibility which must function between semesters in order to carry both student and supervisor through the separating evaluation experience to a deeper, more solid level of relationship in this learning process which asks of both so much self-discipline.

With these two factors in mind, the student's tendency and need to experience change and ending, to feel the letdown and shift of energy before he makes a new beginning, and the necessity of learning to develop in himself the capacity to hold himself steady in offering the professional service, the School may be able to arrange a brief vacation, perhaps a long week-end between semesters, which recognizes the vacation need without interfering with the consistency of agency service. A period of a week or two weeks between semesters, when classes are omitted but work in agency continues, seems to be a helpful device in timing in order to emphasize ending and new beginning without interfering with service to clients. Such a period provides time and opportunity for advisers and teachers to confer with super-

visors on evaluations, and for students who are having problems to confer with advisers. A few students may be dropped
from the School at this time or may leave of their own accord.
An ending process of this final nature requires much extra
time from both adviser and supervisor in coming to a decision and in discussion with the student who is leaving. So
from the point of view of all that the School faculty must
handle at this time, a two-weeks period between semesters
seems none too long.

Strange as it may seem, two weeks without classes does
seem long to students who have become accustomed to the
support of the group and the class discussion in carrying the
training movement. The supervisor who is still seeing the
student in weekly conference during this period should be
aware of the feelings which this change must stir up in the
student. First and most important, she must keep in mind
the deep sense of change due to the experience of evaluation
which they have been through together; in addition, she
must be aware of the uncertainties the student is feeling in
the immediate loss of the class contact and that, however unconsciously, he is beginning to face the requirements of the
second semester ahead.

If the student is able and has made satisfactory progress
in his first semester and if the evaluation has been positive
in character, the supervisor will find it easy to use the assignment of new cases or the pointing up of new problems to be
tackled in his old ones, to serve as a basis for a new hold on
his work. If, however, the student's development has not been
so satisfactory, if his evaluation leaves him unsure and not in
possession of himself or of his skill sufficiently to make a new
beginning in his cases, the supervisor has a more difficult task
in helping him find his own base for a new and more real
start.

But no matter what the ability and achievement of the
student, the supervisor needs to keep before herself in this
mid-semester period the extent to which the fcous of this

training process must be maintained in the student himself as he can find and feel that focus in relation to her and to his clients. So, it seems to me, he should be helped to some expression of how he feels in this between-semester period, particularly in relation to the supervisor who after evaluation inevitably seems new and different. Resting on the development of their capacity to work together in the first semester and on the firm texture of their shared knowledge of the case load, they must learn to work together again on a new level of greater depth and spontaneity. For supervisor as well as student, it is difficult to believe that this relationship can never be taken for granted but must be won again and again at every stage of the process.

CHAPTER X

THE SECOND SEMESTER

Students bring to the first meeting of the second-semester classes a gratifying sense of their greater responsibility for their own learning, a deeper conviction of the purpose for which they are in school. In contrast to the personal beginnings of the first semester each student has a grip on something in agency function, in case load, in his own skill which unites students in classes on a professional basis. It often seems to teachers as if the two-weeks period between semesters had been much longer by the indication of what the student gained in understanding. At the same time the teacher understands the resistance that will be felt to the more difficult requirements set up for the second semester, the deep aversion to the pressure of the form, of the movement itself, which classes emphasize and sustain. These resistances will inevitably find some expression, but this expression can be facilitated by the teacher and made conscious at times in ways that are helpful for the movement of the class as a whole, as well as for the release and additional insight of the individual student. The student's work with clients and his developing skill should rapidly furnish the content as well as the solid base of relationship in class discussion and supervisory conferences throughout the second semester. There is the same rhythm in this semester as in the first: a beginning phase with resistance culminating in a turning point followed by a movement toward evaluation, ending, and plans for the second year. The content in casework in this semester is more extensive and complex than in the first, the student's relation to it more responsible, his understanding, finer, deeper, and more reliable.

The supervisor can take solid satisfaction in the substantial work of her student in this period and can feel indeed that her major contribution has been made, as the student finds so much in his case load to explore, learns from it, and recognizes his own problems in the casework process much more on his own initiative. This is not to imply that the supervisor becomes passive or withholds her own participation in conference discussions. On the other hand, her participation can become freer and more spontaneous as she feels the student's growing strength to be himself, to differ, to oppose, and to find his own function and attitude in the casework relationship. When the student's relation to his client becomes truly and surely his own, his fear of the supervisor's superior skill and knowledge vanishes and he can risk listening, taking in something of what she might have to say about the case, knowing that it is he who will go back into the contact, freed, enriched, and more clearly focused as a result of the conference discussion. If the supervisor loses sight of this increasingly reliable connection between the student and his client, forgets the student, and interposes between herself and the student her own interest in the case, the student will immediately feel this as a threat to his own control and will react against it. He may temporarily lose his hard-won relation to the case and may even drop it in confusion or in negative, impulsive action. The supervisor must be sensitive to his reaction as she finds it in the record of his next contact, or perhaps in his failure to record or to get the material to her. She can feel it, if she is free to, in his attitudes to her in the next conference.

As the supervisor acquires more experience in this process, she will know that in this delicate balance between herself and the student lies the essential skill of supervision. She will guard her own tendency to put in too much of interest, of knowledge, using the reaction of the person she supervises as test of her own activity. She must learn, too, that the student will project his own excessive fear of loss of control in this area where he is still a learner in various ways, and that he may in some moods allow her slightest word to disturb his own relation to his case. Here she must take hold of what is between them fearlessly and vigorously and help him to work through this maze of confusion, through the expression of his resentment against the supervisor, to a clarification of his function and his relationship to his client. This kind of blocking is to be expected again and again in any supervisory relationship and must be resolved as it arises. The supervisee will come through such an experience with deeper and more sensitive awareness of himself and of his place both in the supervisory situation and in the casework situation with his client. He will gain greater understanding and conviction about the meaning of help, the struggle against taking it, and the strength required to give it.

This new strength in the student wrested out of struggle and directed into his relations with his client is the basic force which moves toward a true ending of this supervisory relationship and of his first-year learning experience. He knows as a rule that he will leave this supervisor and this case load, and perhaps the agency where he has been a student. If he has gained the strength and skill required to continue in training, he will go on to a second year which will be different in many aspects from the one he has come through successfully.

The time structure of the School provides the dates for evaluation with the supervisor, for discussion of his work as a whole and of the point he has reached in training with teachers and adviser, and finally sets a time for planning for his second-year placement with the teacher in charge of such placements. These structures serve to objectify the student's reactions to ending and put within his reach the tangible, concrete steps which he can take in making his training process a continuing one in which his will can engage more actively and really.

But it must never be forgotten that this conclusion of the first year of professional training is for every individual student an ending experienced more deeply and more consciously than he has ever experienced this aspect of living in his life before, unless he has been exposed to analytic therapy.

Supervisors and teachers carry this awareness more deeply than the students. Their experience and discipline enable them to detach themselves enough to permit the student's feelings and attitudes in ending to be fully realized and expressed. These run the gamut from fear, guilt, and a sense of loss, from regret and pain, to relief and satisfaction, even to the extreme of triumphant fullness, in the realization of the independent self. There will be negative feelings, too, perhaps some destructive attitudes or behavior in the student's struggle to free himself. Something in the old self and the situation now fast becoming old must be left behind to make way for the new organization. In this final stage the supervisor has to be prepared to receive some projection of what the student needs to abandon. It is not uncommon for the student filled with the guilt of separation to bring out in his final evaluation conference some criticism of her, to refer to help she failed to give. He does this impulsively and blindly as an expression of the negative feelings so sharply felt in this ending experience. For the supervisor, related to the whole value and meaning of the experience and aware of all she has given throughout, this criticism is hard to take, particularly so as it is often located on so slight a point, without rhyme or reason in the total relationship. But take it she must, for if she should attempt to argue it, to make it take its rightful place, she will only give the student occasion to falsify the relationship further. The only thing that enables her to take it is her conviction that she has made her contribution and that the student's essential and difficult task now is to end with her as best he can. He must save some difference for himself, some advantage that is his, on which to extricate himself from the relationship. The richer the person, the deeper the experience, the freer he will be to feel not only the reward of his own fuller use of himself but gratitude to the other person, the teacher or the supervisor, who has enabled him to have this experience.

Chapter XI

THE SECOND YEAR OF TRAINING

The long intermission of three months between the end of the first year and the beginning of the second year of training in the professional school which operates on the semester time plan is an important and valuable part of the two-year educational experience. That the student regards it as such is indicated by the fact that not even the youngest student often has an inclination to return to the summer jobs in camp or other situations which had meaning and importance for him before he entered the professional school. Nor does the student feel that it is desirable or appropriate to take a three-months summer vacation. Even the youngest student has left behind the college student pattern and has become identified with a working, earning, professional group. Of his own accord, as well as at the dictate of the school, he seeks a job in a social agency with salary attached.

The School, since it is not in formal classwork session, cannot undertake to control or direct these summer placements in any way beyond the part it has already taken in planning the student's second-year placement. By the end of the first year in early June most of these placements are arranged. Student, School, and fieldwork agency have each participated actively in this placement.[1] The student has made a

[1] For a description of this second-year placement process, the following statement from the catalogue will serve:
"Admission to Second Year
"Students who have completed the first year in the School are eligible to apply for second year. This group includes students who are currently enrolled in the first year and those who have previously completed the first year. . . .
"Current first-year students discuss plans for a second year with their faculty advisers in April. Former students applying for readmission also file applications in the Spring. In accepting a student for the second year, the School is influenced both by the quality of his work in the first year and by the availability of an appropriate field placement. In general, the second year

choice among available agencies, the agency executive in conference with the student has chosen the student, has offered him a second-year placement. A summer plan for the student will offer itself naturally, either out of the first-year fieldwork placement or out of the second. Sometimes both agencies want the student for summer work, and he must choose between them, but in either case it is understood to be a limited job for so many weeks under conditions and supervision provided by the agency and without School controls. In every way, the difference between this working experience and the learning experience of the School year must be emphasized. The student will resist the difference to some extent but to a greater degree he welcomes this opportunity to feel himself a working member of a staff, to earn a salary, to do a real job in job terms.

It is no wonder that students returning to the second-year curriculum in October seem to have grown many inches in professional stature. They bring back a firmer identification with the profession, a surer sense of themselves as professional people. Each has much to tell of his summer work and welcomes the opportunity to share his experience with his fellow students. There is an immediate feeling of unity in a second-year practice class, a unity which had to be

---

immediately follows the first. For some students, a year or more of paid employment in an agency before completing training is advisable.
"Plans for Second Year
"A student may undertake the second year of study according to one of the following plans:
"1. Agency fellowship. Fellowships covering tuition and minimum living expenses offered by agencies are available for outstanding students. In offering these fellowships, the School and the agencies take into consideration the quality of work done by the student in the first year, and the amount and type of his current and previous experience.
"2. Agency placement without fellowship. Under this arrangement, students bear the total cost of training.
"3. Work-study plan. Students may apply to complete their training as part-time paid members of field-work agency staffs, providing the agency insures the student adequate supervision acceptable to the School, at least one day a week free from job for classes, suitable adjustment of work load, and access to agency material for a thesis." (Pennsylvania School of Social Work, *Catalogue Issue*, 1947-48, pp. 23-24.)

worked for through many long weeks of first-year class discussions. But this positive return to the training process by
no means describes the whole picture. While each and every
student has chosen to return, is truly identified with the
School and the profession, and has engaged his will deeply
in this learning process, at the same time he resists this
return with greater strength than he did the original beginning, for now he knows, as he did not know before, how,
much is asked of him in this process. If the summer has
given him an opportunity to use what he has already learned
freely and effectively, he will surely feel that he has enough.
No further change should be required of him. But he cannot
completely blot out the stirrings of awareness that more is
required or he would not be returning to the School. If he
feels his first-year struggle to have been a very painful one,
he may come to the second year determined that it shall
not happen to him again.

For all students beginning again in the second year, the
imminence of ending, embodied in the thesis requirement
of the second semester, looms up more fearfully than ending
in the first year, both in its finality and in the skill and independent work it must evidence. They have studied the
thesis case material of students who have gone before them,
and they have heard many rumors of the difficulty of the
thesis assignment from graduates. "Will I be ready for it or
equal to it?" is a haunting question. They handle it in different ways. Some students enter the second year with a
thesis topic already in mind; others shy away from the
mention of the word. It is the difficult task of teacher and
supervisor to get through the seeming positive unity of the
class group, the independence and ego assertions unconsciously but forcefully set against learning, to a new beginning, for the class as a whole and for each and every student.

The supervisor of the second-year student should be, and
usually is, an experienced supervisor. If she has already had
experience with second-year students, she knows before she

begins of the life blood that must go into this struggle, her own as well as the student's. There is no way to remain aloof and untouched even if she would save herself, for what the student has already experienced in a first year means that in a second he will put a demand on supervision for all that he needs to see him through a deeper process of change and reorganization to a surer use of himself in skillful service to the client. This demand may express itself in resistance and may fight every inch of the way and admission of what it needs and wants. But we assume that fundamentally the will-to-change must be operative or the student would not be in his second year. Sometimes, of course, a mistake has been made; he is not able to see through his choice. Then teachers and supervisors must help him to leave but this should be a rare occurrence if the first-year evaluations, choices, and decisions have been soundly made.

When the student begins his second-year fieldwork assignment with his second-year supervisor, he may be starting in a new agency or a new department of agency. If he is in the same agency working from the function he learned to use to a degree in his first year, there will be at any rate a change in case load. For every student the feeling of newness in himself and in his relation to a new supervisor, new teachers, new classes, is made real and actual in relation to the clients where he must find his function all over again. The wise supervisor knows that she must struggle with the student in his efforts to get hold of something familiar in the situation against his tendencies to control it all in his own terms. Since he feels all change so acutely, she can help him by pointing up the actual concrete differences in this second-year placement; he has a new supervisor, a new case load; perhaps both agency and function are new to him. Some aspects of this difference he will dislike and fight; the sooner and the more freely he can be helped to express his feeling, the more quickly the relationship can move into a more positive ability to work together on the cases.

Here in the case load the second-year student, no matter how much experience he brings, must be helped, as the first-year student must be helped, to get down to the actual beginning with the particular, individual client. The supervisor knows well the vagueness and generality that pervade the early conference discussions before this real beginning has been achieved. Her rightful impatience with it, if nothing else, will speed her effort to cut through it, to bring out the student's expression of his genuine negative feelings. Only when these have been fully expressed and truly placed on something in supervision or in school is the student free to take them back into himself as the natural reactions to change that they really are. Then and then only he is able to get to the client.

I can find no better way to make vivid the sense of change and newness which a student feels at the beginning of second year than to quote from a student's statement in her thesis. This student in her early twenties came into the professional school direct from college and made fine progress in her first year of training in the long-time care department of a child-placing agency. Her second-year placement was in the same agency in the reception department, where her case load was to consist of babies placed in temporary homes. She had learned well the function, philosophy, and practice of this agency as she had been the worker for some of its children already placed in permanent foster homes. But what a different problem faces her when she herself must actually receive the baby into care at the moment of separation from his mother and go into the foster home with him in a placement process which is temporary, leading to another separation, a permanent placement later! She says:

I never sought for a way of helping more earnestly than when I entered the reception department of the X Child Placing Agency as a second-year student and found that I was being asked to implement a movement toward separation between a baby and a temporary foster mother. The framework with which I was presented was the placement of babies in temporary foster homes with a view to removing them when a more stable plan for their future was reached. Abstracted from the whole configuration of the baby's life situation, this practice seemed to me an almost impossible one for baby and foster mother to bear. What I knew of the external factors that led my agency to use such a practice, though real, could not in itself bring me to a true acceptance of the practice. The conviction I lacked was that this procedure could provide a growth-producing experience for baby and foster mother. Without such a conviction I could hardly assume my role as a helping person within this framework. I needed a deeper understanding of the use of this structure before I could accept it as providing a growth experience for the baby needing foster care, and I needed to know how it is possible for anyone to separate from a deeply meaningful relationship.

She achieved this conviction in her second-year training experience and states its basis and identifies the experience out of which she reached it in another paragraph in the thesis.

Essential to being helpful is the conviction that an individual has the capacity to live through this precarious experience. We gain such a conviction only from living through a parallel experience ourselves, for in understanding our own movement through it, we become aware of our own strength and of the help we received. This knowledge of our own struggle is the only instruction we can trust, affirm, and use in helping another.

This depth and clarity of conviction can be reached only when an experience in a helping relationship has been lived through to an ending in the self. So this statement could only be written in the second and final semester of training in the form of a thesis that represents the eventuation of the training experience. To a greater or lesser degree, depending on individual depth and capacity, each student must come to this conviction and by means of a similar experience of his own internal struggle.

For this student, the struggle was focused in the painful

problem of separation with which she was faced by her new function and in her relation to her supervisor. The foster-home placement offered her everything she could desire; the supervisor was ready and equipped to give everything she could ask for her second-year experience, of warmth, of understanding, of strength and supervisory skill. In direct proportion to the strength of her own need for the experience she might find in the second year, her very resistance to becoming involved in it necessarily organized her overt activity against it. She came back to school in October with a program of extracurricular activities planned for herself, calculated to protect her from too much involvement in class- and fieldwork. Not many conferences had taken place before her supervisor detected the barrier which the student had thrown up between them, and the frank discussion of the student's fears led to a complete revision of her extra-curricular program. Once this initial resistance was overcome, the student threw herself into her cases and into the conference discussions with her characteristic sensitivity and intensity. Her learning was rapid; her understanding fine in quality. The cases provided a full variety of experience to give her all she needed of deepened and extended understanding of this problem of the child's capacity to use a temporary situation for his own growth, of what the agency and the worker must put in to help him.

But this student's own problem in relationship was carried to a deeper and more precarious level for her when she herself faced the midyear evaluation and the end of the practice class with all that it foreshadowed of the final ending of the school training and the separation from student supervision. Here she fought actively with a strength she had never known she possessed, and found herself capable of destructive behavior and bitter feeling inconsistent with her picture and ideal of herself. This struggle was a matter of weeks, painful in its nature for the adviser, the supervisor, and the teachers involved in it with her. Her foster parents and babies suffered too during this period no doubt, but less than the other people concerned since, for her clients, she kept her professional relationship under the discipline she had already achieved. It delayed her thesis until the middle of the second semester when she came through the negative phase of her separation to an acceptance of herself in this process. The self that she achieves in this process, as she herself states in what I have already quoted, has a new maturity and in its use now with foster parents and babies she is in possession of the understanding of relationship, movement, and separation on which true ability to help must rest.

While this student may have a greater awareness of her own process than some others and more capacity to articulate it, she is not exceptional in her conviction about the nature of the process itself and in her possession of her own experience in it. Every student in his own individual terms must experience this process of change and growth in himself and must know it and affirm it as the basis of his understanding of his client's problem in using the service of the agency.

One more illustration of the second-year learning experience of a student will have value in illustrating further the nature of this process. In contrast to the student already quoted, this student brought maturity of age and experience to her training. She was in her late thirties, with some years in social work and with experience in an allied field in an executive capacity. It was obvious at once that she was an extremely intelligent, thoughtful person, thorough, logical and well organized in her thinking, and dignified and reserved in relations with others. While her progress in the first year was substantial and solid, her teachers recognized in her aloofness and tendency toward rigidity, attitudes which she would need to change if she were to reach the full and free use of her able self in helpfulness to her clients. The fieldwork placement arranged for her second year offered the possibility for the experience she needed if she could use it, an agency well organized and administered, a function new and challenging, a supervisor sensitive, mature, and skillful.

The supervisor[2] has analyzed this training experience in her own record from which I quote.

Student impressed me as a thoroughly responsible person with a great deal of strength and integrity. The school of social work described her as thoughtful and sensitive with a pleasing personality, which could not but make itself felt. She had completed a very productive first year of training and was considered as having excellent potentialities for casework. The school's very acceptance of her as of fellowship caliber was a recognition of her capacities. It was felt that she still had a great deal to learn, especially in the area of leaving to the client that which is his part in the helping process.

From the beginning, she had been eager to work in a children's agency. She likes children and brought to this experience a strong identification with the child. She felt the pain in placement, that is, in separation, keenly, but had sufficient strength and identification with the service to carry through responsibly with the client to the end. At times her identification with the child and a too-ready acceptance of placement as a solution to the problems inherent in difficult parent-child relationships led her to over-identify with the child against the parent.

Her very strength and determination, that is, the use she made of it, created difficutly for her in her work with clients as well as in supervision. She is by nature a very reserved person, one who does not find it easy to share her feelings. Beyond this, she seemed to exert an iron control and discipline over herself, which gave her work at times an aspect of stiltedness, of flatness rather than one of dimension and depth. In her interviews with clients she did not let her own feelings come through and thus was not always able to help the client with his feelings. This was particu-

2 I regret exceedingly that I cannot give credit to the supervisor whose work and thinking I am using here. To identify her would be to identify the student, who herself a supervisor now, might well object to the publication of her learning struggle, although she has consented to its use here. I have taken every precaution, therefore, to disguise her identity without in any way altering essential facts or factors in the process.

larly noticeable in her lack of awareness of ambivalence as an ever present factor in the process of taking help and especially so in the taking of help around placement of one's child. The decision to place one's child is rarely arrived at wholeheartedly by the client, but is fraught with guilt, indecision, feelings of inadequacy, and a painful recognition of the individual's difference from his fellow men. There was a quality of literalness about her which made her take whatever the client might say at the moment as something that was whole or right for him. She became confused and frustrated when the next moment the client seemingly reversed himself. Her conception of feeling had an aspect of totality and singleness. She found it difficult to experience it in parts for herself and for her clients and she could not bear the fluidity that there is in all casework helping. With this, she took over too much for the client and carried too great a feeling of responsibility and stake for the outcome of her work with him. Her use of structure, too, had this element of finality in it. If the client balked at a particular piece of structure such as a necessary contact with the Department of Welfare or working out financial arrangements, she would view this with finality as proof of his not wanting to go ahead with placement, rather than to see what the struggle over this point signified for him and to help him move beyond it toward a more integrated decision for himself.

While some of this is typical of all beginning learning in casework, there ran through it, nevertheless, a thread that was student's own unique relationship to helping and to taking help. Since feeling held such totality for her, she was afraid of it. She could not bring her feelings out in supervision any more than she did in her relationships with her clients. When I discussed her work, she looked downcast. I tried to bring out her feelings about taking help. I felt it was not easy for her, who had been an executive, used to giving orders, to have to take instead. At her stage of development, too, she must have arrived at some acceptable way of life for herself. Was she afraid that this would mean too much change for her? She could not accept understanding from me at this point. She could only affirm the part in her that wanted help. Her reaction to criticism and taking help, she felt, was a universal one. Naturally anybody would rather have praise.

She felt, however, that her very going to school was an acceptance of her role as a learner. She valued my help and wanted to learn. I did not doubt it. I knew she was putting a great deal into this training experience and I respected her for it. Yet I knew that learning could not always take place positively. It had a negative and painful side. Could she let that part of her feeling come through here with me? She was suspicious, she said, of what she calls "trusting to feeling." The school and I emphasized this so much. She thought a social worker would be disciplined in her feelings. So did I, but said this could only take place professionally, if one let oneself know and experience one's feelings. She, I felt, was withholding hers. She argued with me on this point, instancing illustrations of destruction being wrought in the world under the name of free expression of feeling. I said her illustrations seemed extreme and very far removed from what we were experiencing together here and now. Wasn't she struggling with me right now and could she feel that? I knew she had had many experiences that made her fearful of feeling and I recognized her right to personal reserve, but I thought she did not know what the school and I were talking about, namely, about a freer, more creative use of herself in her casework and a letting go of that tightness and control. I knew that she was capable of deep feeling. She has such very nice feeling for people. Could she dare let some of it come through? Of course, she knew what I was talking about, we had gone over it when discussing instances in her work where her problem showed itself. She could see a little, too, how she was fighting me.

While she was fighting, there was at the same time a kind of determination about her wanting to learn. She kept her conference periods with me scrupulously and always brought her case material in time to discuss it in conference. Part of her undoubtedly wanted help, and she was eager to get ahead and to develop professionally. Even while she struggled against change, some change did take place. So much of her work was sensitive, especially where she could identify more readily, for instance in situations where the need for placement was caused by external reasons, such as illness. She was utterly responsible as to every detail of the job and carried this professional attitude beyond her immediate case load. This, together with great concern and interest in general social welfare, reflected her deep identification with the field and her acceptance of her own role in it.

As time went on she began to have less of a stake in placement as such, recognizing that while it might help with the immediate situation, it did put into motion an entirely new set of problems. With this, she could leave the client freer to make his own decision. She began to be aware of how great a part ambivalence plays in the application process. She also used structure more imaginatively and altogether began to get a better hold of the intake job. We were both naturally pleased with her development. Yet in the one essential area of using herself more spontaneously, in just being able to "be with" the client in his feeling, change came slowly and hard. She was still struggling with that aspect of her development and part of her was holding itself back from yielding to learning.

In school, too, she was fighting. This expressed itself in struggling with the philosophy for which the school stands, accepting some of it, yet holding herself aloof from its very essence. She brought some of this struggle into her supervisory conferences and at first I was quite willing to talk with her about it, thinking that she was trying to find herself in relation to the casework philosophy taught at the school. However, it soon became clear that she was arguing with me and that I could not let it continue. Her struggle with learning was projected onto me and while that was all right as far as it went, it did not go far enough. It remained too external. I let her alone for a while, that is, I did not initiate a discussion of anything problematic in her work with me, so as to give her a chance to work on it by herself. But this did not bring much change. She could see what was wrong in her work, was dissatisfied, but seemed to have reached a blocking in her learning beyond which she could not go. Something decisive had to happen now, something that would shake her out of that rut she was in.

I arranged for a special evaluation conference and told her that I thought she was struggling against all learning at this point. While her work on the whole was not bad, in many instances, was even quite good, she had not made essential progress with what I considered her problem as a caseworker. Unless there were some decisive change, before the end of the semester,

I could not give her fieldwork credit for the semester. (This was done in consultation with the adviser at the school.) This would be on the basis of her not approximating her own capacity. She became a little defiant and said with an edge in her voice, "Perhaps you overestimate my capacities." I said, "Perhaps I do." With this, she had to fight me a little bit more, and said that she for one believed in discipline and in being in control of oneself at all times. I thought that that was all right if that was what she wanted, except that it stood in the way of her becoming a caseworker. She was really quite mad now and said, "Well there are other things besides casework." I said, "Yes, and these other things may not require as much of the self in the way of change as does casework." At this point I didn't know whether she could change or whether she wanted to. With a shrug of the shoulders, she said that neither did she.

She was visibly upset during this discussion, but would not give in to her feelings. She went on to discuss some cases with me as if nothing had happened. I felt I had to help her see what it was she was doing just here with me in the way of exerting control, and how this tended to cut herself off and shut out the other person. I told her that I was amazed at her being able to go on to a discussion of her cases and to act as if she was as unconcerned with what we had talked about. I told her frankly that I, in her place, would not have been able to do this. After all we had talked about some pretty serious matters. I knew how much of herself she had invested in this training experience and at what cost and sacrifice. I knew she could not but feel concerned. Her first reaction to this was, "Well, you told me, and now I know." But then she yielded, broke down, and cried, half letting it be that way, and half fighting it. "What's there in it for me," she demanded, "in thus losing control?" I could not tell her what meaning it would have for her, except perhaps that she had dared to let it be. After crying for a time she walked out of the room, slamming the door behind her. I knew how painful this conference must have been for her and I thought she was certainly entitled to feel hurt and indignant at me at a time like this.

At our next conference I asked her how she felt and how things were going with her. In response, she handed me a paper she had written for school, saying that I might just as well read it, since I was in it too. This was a paper on feeling, the pain in it for her, and how she had tried to protect herself from pain by building a wall around herself. Now she was fighting anything which threatened to tear down the wall. The paper described the feeling of separation and utter isolation caused by this withdrawal of herself, the fear for her in it, either way, that is, in change as well as in remaining within her shell. The paper was beautifully written reflecting the depth of her feeling and the degree to which she was stirred and shaken.

I commented on this and said that it would be hard to forgive me for having aroused her so. This she acknowledged readily. On the other hand, she could now see the relationship of what she was experiencing with me to what had been blocking her in her casework. She felt that she also could understand her clients better. I said I thought that was important and I was willing to wait and see where all this took her.

At one point during this period, student worked with an adolescent girl who was in a rebellious phase of development. In describing the girl to me, she talked with great glee of how negatively the girl, Bella, was related to all authority at this point. She said very wholeheartedly, "I like Bella." I said that I thought that there was a little "Bella" in her right now in relation to me. We both laughed and understood each other.

During the next few conferences she was much more sharing and was willing to let me in on what she was feeling. She told me that she had dealt with the painful experiences in her life by blotting them out of her memory and by not letting herself feel. Her feelings, she said, could reach such violent pitch that she was afraid of them, and so she tried to control them through sheer effort of will. I asked whether this was really bringing her the inner peace she wanted. She could see that it did not. I thought that one could not get rid of the past by merely denying it. Perhaps she could gain a new inner balance not through denial but through taking possession of her feeling, the good and the bad of it, through letting the past live, and herself outlive it, as it were.

All of this marked a very difficult period for this student. It seemed to her as if she were drifting and at loose ends. To her, who had always been so in control of herself, this was upsetting and disturbing. Yet this was just what she needed—to yield and give in to herself. I am sure she knew I was in it together with her. The school was in it too, and she found her contacts with her adviser extremely helpful to her during this difficult phase of her development.

Throughout this period, even while she felt so unmoored, there was a new direction in her casework. I am quoting from my evaluation of her, written at the end of the school semester:

"The change in her casework has been remarkable. She now uses herself creatively with the client and is able to let the fine feeling she has for people come through dynamically in her contacts with them. Feeling no longer holds so much totality and finality for her. She is able to be more tentative with her clients and able to bear the tentativeness in them and in the case situation. Above all, she now has a deep conviction of the client's part and she not only is willing for it to be that way, but is also developing skill in freeing the client to participate fully. She is able to sustain a process with the client, and the ending phase of her contacts is as meaningful as the beginning. She is generally freer and more relaxed and it is good to see the pleasure and confidence she derives from her own movement.

". . . I feel that the student has unusual potentialities as a caseworker and that the movement she has made during the latter part of the semester, certainly warrants my recommending her for full casework credit for the term."

Recently she had a client, a young girl who had a baby born out of wedlock. The client found it extremely difficult to share her feelings with student and did not want to talk about her experience, trying to deny to herself the reality of it. Student was most sympathetic with the girl. In one of her interviews when they were discussing the situation, she tried to help her see that one could not get rid of the past by denying it. These were the very words I had used with her. When she told me about it, I searched her face for a sign of recognition, but there was none, so much had she made this her own.

Now that the school year is drawing to a close, she is reviewing for herself what this entire school experience has meant to her. She is amazed at how much she has been able to change. She had not thought it possible at her age. I felt that it was what she had brought to the experience and what she had been willing to put into it that had enabled her to change as much as she had. She said it was wonderful to feel that she had "come through." This was giving her courage and confidence in her work with clients. They, too, can "come through." The school experience has been very meaningful for her and at present she is feeling the pain in ending keenly. She now lets herself experience feeling, and she can live with it.

This record of a second-year training experience needs no comment beyond the fine, sensitive analysis inherent in the supervisor's thinking throughout her description of the process. The supervisor's point of view, her activity, and her thinking are as clearly set forth as is the student's problem and part in the process. But I should like to draw from the record of the training of this one student several points which I believe fundamental to all training for social casework on the second-year level.

A record of an experience which penetrates so deeply into the very center of the self will inevitably raise the familiar question: Where do supervision and training leave off and where does therapy begin? I put the question in this form purposely because it is the form in which it usually takes shape and which implies in itself the fallacy, as I see it, of the basic conception of personality and personality change which underlies it. It implies a static and structural picture of personality organization and development and also the possibility of control both by the helper and the one who seeks help through an assumed ability to determine process, to decide what levels of personality will be touched and what will be kept safe and intact. This is exactly the point of view which this able, intelligent student brings to training, opposing it with all her strength to the point of view of School and supervisor. She is willing, more than that, determined, to use her logical, analytical mind to learn what she must in this professional field, but her feelings are her own. They are deep and powerful. She has learned to control them in ways that make living possible for her, in ways that make her an admirable character. She values her life adjustment and it would violate her conception of herself, her ideal for her development, to seek therapy. Nor would the supervisor or the School conceive of suggesting it to her. They, too, admire the fine personal adjustment this student has achieved and would have no reason and no justification for touching it except in a training relationship.

It is essential to an understanding of this training process to see that the question of whether this is therapy or supervision never presents itself to School, supervisor, or student for the reason that the distinction is so clear from the beginning in the function which determines all that happens in the process. If a school accepts the function of training students to help clients who come in search of this help from agency services, it is obligated to ask each student to meet the requirement of that training. This necessitates for each a new experiencing of his responses, his feelings, his attitudes, and his behavior, in new situations; inevitably it requires change in his personality structure. How deep this change will go can never be predicted. It can only be pointed out step by step in the process as teacher or supervisor becomes aware of the problem that the student's attitude is creating in relation to his client.

The student's attitude can often be handled partially in his relation to the particular client or in his immediate feelings about supervision, as we have seen in the illustrations of the beginning experiences of first-year students. But on the second-year level of training for many, perhaps for a majority of students, there comes a point when the need for more fundamental change is indicated. Perhaps it arises inevitably to a certain degree for all students from the very nature of the process itself. Their experience is on a deeper level in the second year, more difference has been taken in, and a final ending is approaching. Teacher and supervisor on the one side, student on the other, feel deeply the sense of focus which this final ending creates between them. One can only describe this as a training movement, with its own function, timing, structure, focus, and goal, clearly differentiated from therapy. It resembles therapy in results only to the extent that the laws of personality change and growth are basic in both processes.

The personality problem which the student quoted presents to training is no different from the problem she would have presented to therapy if it had been within her range of possible action to seek therapeutic help. The reason for challenging her adjustment in training is to acquire a skill, not to correct a personality adjustment. The possibility of change in this problem lies in the question of whether she can give up any of her own already-established ego ideal, her will and previous direction, her current organization of herself, sufficiently to accept something new, foreign, and different. At first this comes at her as invasion by the School's point of view. It requires her to admit the reality of the feeling which she has both fought and denied and to accept the validity of expressing it if she wants to attain the training goal which she herself has chosen.

The supervisor's ability to accept and sustain the painful responsibility of requiring the student to effect some change in this fundamental organization of herself is clearly seen to be rooted in her twofold responsibility for clients and for student, focused as a single responsibility for the student's training movement. She sees the student's problem in her records, in her inability to feel the ambivalent negative forces in the parent's movement toward placement. She knows that the student cannot become an effective caseworker unless she learns to recognize these forces and to respond to them. She knows also that the student's blind spots in relation to her clients are directly connected with her refusal to recognize these feelings in herself as they are deeply stirred by her positive movement into the training experience. The supervisor attempts first to give specific recognition to the student's problem in her cases, and makes every effort to penetrate the student's resistance, to help her see that she is fighting her and the School. Some students less tightly organized might have come through this period with sufficient change and recognition of problem to meet the constantly held-to requirement that they move forward in ability to use themselves more freely and with greater discipline in behalf of the client. But while this student does seem to make some progress in her casework, in the careful, considered judgment of adviser and supervisor it is not sufficient. One might argue that she will get it later in working experience. But to leave it to that, for the supervisor who is in this experience with her, would be an evasion of what is between them, a refusal to give her the completely honest judgment that, if this is the best she can do, she is handicapped in her chosen profession. In proportion to her own ability and integrity, this student is entitled to an equal degree of honesty of judgment from those responsible for her training; the supervisor from her own integrity and professional maturity can give her no less.

Only the keenest sense of professional difference and the deepest conviction of responsibility to use it to the utmost in behalf of the student can bring a supervisor to the difficult point of action described in the record as follows: "I arranged for a special evaluation conference and told her . . . she had not made essential progress with what I considered her problem as a caseworker. Unless there were some decisive change, before the end of the semester, I could not give her fieldwork credit for the semester."

The authority inherent in this supervisory action is inescapable. It feels harsh and arbitrary to the reader as it does to the student while she is still fighting it. But it is no more than the gathering-together into one point of focus of the authority implicit in all training which asks the student to meet and take into himself an essential difference that requires change in himself. Even the most external educational standard and requirement contain the "you must learn this or else." At any point it may be opposed by the student so that this edge of difference as requirement is felt as sharply as it is felt here between this supervisor and this second-year student.

One has only to look at the negative attitudes that typically oppose themselves to the teacher in school or college in order to realize the extent to which this edge of authoritative difference is feared and evaded. Only the most responsible teachers learn to use it consciously in behalf of the student; only the rarest student in relationship with the rare teacher goes all the way in experiencing what is there to be experienced if this crisis is used, not evaded. This authority asks that one yield to the other's difference, to his superior professional development, to his greater knowledge and skill. The very word "yield" carries the meaning which must be resisted in some degree by everyone, particularly by the strong-willed, independent, well-organized person. One must experience yielding truly and deeply as at bottom a potentiality for growth in the own self in order to be free of the fear of dependence, of weakness, of loss of self, which haunts every individual in his movement into relationship.

The clear, fine line between personal and professional is obliterated at this point where difference meets difference so sharply. For at this point of impact, the self is driven back to its organic and impulsive sources and becomes total in its reactions. This experience which, for the supervisor, can only be undertaken out of professional function and responsibility must feel to the student purely personal. If he can give up his willful resistance and yield to the other, it is actually a yielding of the whole self, totally unlike the limited giving-in on a specific point, which leaves the self intact, wholly different from adjusting to a particular external requirement.

Because this yielding is a total emotional experience, felt as personal, that is, as individual and unlimited, the student's reaction will necessarily extend it to the supervisor. In its very quality and essence it is a uniting experience enhanced by the sense of the difference it has overcome. The student must resent the fact that his personal experience is not for the supervisor what it is for himself and he may set himself to make it so. At the same time, his strongest guarantee that this experience will eventuate for him in gain, rather than loss of self, lies in the supervisor's ability to hold to her professional difference throughout this experience. It is her capacity to do this that sets the professional limits for the movement of his powerful feelings, which he now truly knows as ambivalent. As a result they move back into the relationship with the client with new freedom, strength, and sensitivity to the client's ambivalence. The School, too, has an important part in keeping this relationship always three cornered. It is interesting to see in the record of this second-year student that she found it possible to express the depth of her feeling only indirectly in a paper for her teacher which, however, she manages to share with the supervisor.

If the supervisor has not achieved the maturity and skill to maintain her difference in this process naturally, in behalf of the student, if she must assert this edge of authority arbitrarily and withhold her recognition of the student's reaction to it, the student will not be able to get the full experience of yielding wholeheartedly to all his feelings as was the privilege of the student whose experience we have quoted. One senses in every word of the record this supervisor's warmth of feeling for what the student was going through, her fine identification with every shade of feeling. As she says: "The student was not alone in this. I am sure she knew that I was in it. The School was in it too."

From an impact with the sustained and necessary difference of the professional person who carries the training requirement responsibly and skillfully, the student who comes through it learns the fundamental dynamics of a helping process from having experienced them. He becomes aware of his own natural ambivalence in taking help, the fear of loss of control, of involvement in relationship which inhibits his own movement, the strength of negative resistance which fights his own positive will-to-learn and to yield. He has felt the firmness of the other person's authority, holding him to the necessity of movement throughout his struggle with sensitivity and consideration for all his feelings. He discovers that he can "come through" this struggle with gain rather than loss of self.

For any student to know these dynamics in his own struggle to use help is to know also the client's struggle. Parallel with his own movement in taking help goes the release of his capacity to accept not only his own feelings, but those of the client. At the same time, he is achieving the discipline of his feelings which permits the client to have and to come through this experience of choice and change with the student as helper. As the student in the quoted record says: "It was wonderful to feel that she had 'come through.' This was giving her courage and confidence in her work with clients. They, too, can 'come through.'"

CHAPTER XII

THE THESIS AS THE ENDING PHASE OF THE TWO-YEAR TRAINING PROCESS

The thesis project taken over from academic education when the Pennsylvania School became affiliated with the University of Pennsylvania in 1935 has become, in the course of its use in this two-year professional curriculum, the most effective structure that could have been devised for a true realization and eventuation of the whole training movement. The catalogue description gives a simple factual statement of the nature of the requirement. To quote:

Thesis

Candidates for the degree of Master of Social Work or for the Vocational Certificate complete a substantial discussion of a professional problem arising within their own practice. The problem is chosen and developed in consultation with a thesis adviser, usually the staff instructor most closely related to the field of specialization. In all cases the agency in which the student is doing field work must approve the choice of material.[1]

This statement differentiates the thesis project of the Pennsylvania School of Social Work from the typical research thesis by the requirement that the thesis must develop out of the student's own practice instead of in the use of materials gathered from records or from experience other than his own.

In order to qualify for the thesis work, the student must have demonstrated in the first semester of his second year of practice some basic understanding of the meaning of a functional helping process and the beginnings of a professional use of himself in such a process with his clients. The supervisor's record, quoted in the preceding chapter, shows the extent of the challenge that the responsible supervisor

[1] Pennsylvania School of Social Work, *Catalogue Issue*, 1947-48, p. 25.

felt it necessary to present to that able student to help her to break through her inhibitions to use herself fully in the helping process. It shows, also, the careful, serious, and continuous process between supervisor and adviser by which the student's change and learning and her skill in practice were evaluated. It is on this progress that the student's readiness to undertake the thesis work rests. While the School recognizes the supervisor's essential role in bringing the student's learning to this level, it is clear that the supervisor should not be asked to go beyond the point of giving credit for the fieldwork of the semester in her evaluation and that the full responsibility of decision as to the student's readiness to undertake the thesis work must rest with the School.

In this final semester of training, therefore, of which the thesis work is the center, while the three-way relationship of School, supervisor, and student continues, the role of each in this relationship alters radically. The student must effect a certain separation from his supervisor and does naturally do this in the evaluation process which takes place between them at the end of the first semester. He must separate to some extent from the day-by-day ongoing connection with his case load in order to analyze part of that experience as thesis material. He enters, then, into a semester of work with a thesis adviser in the School, usually the same adviser who has been his casework teacher and adviser in the first semester. Whether she is familiar or strange to him, the student makes her and this thesis assignment into a new and strange undertaking in which he recapitulates his whole training experience and through it finds and organizes his new professional self in its basic convictions and its skill in practice.

When the student registers for his thesis project at the beginning of the second semester of his second year, he is given in writing a detailed description of the time structure and procedures under which he will work. There is a date for submitting his title and for discussion of it with his ad-

viser, a date for working on his outline, a date for handing
in the case material, a date for a final rough draft, and one
for the completed bound thesis copy. In all, about six appointments with his thesis adviser are indicated and set up
roughly in time.

The thesis adviser who accepts responsibility for carrying
the student through the thesis work faces, first of all, the
obligation to involve the student in using her help on the
thesis against his temptation to escape this process by returning to his supervisor who knows his cases as well as he
does. A major problem at the same time is to help him assert
the validity of his own experience with his clients against
his tendency to deny that he has anything to write about. It
must be there in his records or he would not be certified to
begin the work on the thesis but it is the rare student who
can move easily into a choice of thesis problem, a statement
of title, a selection of case material. Some students bring too
much, others too little. Characteristically, students start with
generalizations and must learn to break this down in order to
get to the concrete and real in their own experience. They
feel hampered by all that has been better said by other
students before them or they tend to rely completely on what
has been written by the faculty and must be challenged to
bring out in their own words the essential bases for their
thinking. Much of this is no different from the process that
anyone goes through in attempting to state in organized
written form for the first time the conclusions of his own
experience and thinking. The significant difference in the
writing process of the students in this school of social work
is that it is undertaken and carried through in a helping
process with a professional person, the adviser, in a definite
and limited time structure. It is therefore essentially of the
same nature as the other learning processes of the preceding
semesters. It does not stand alone but is an integral part and
a true ending phase of the total training movement. In the
limited time unit of this one semester of work with its half-

dozen appointments with an adviser, the student in taking such specific and defined help comes to a clearer understanding of his own pattern of using help and of the typical struggle and ambivalence of any human being in this process. In his writing he sees himself more objectively in his relation to his clients and gains greater capacity to evaluate his own skill. The final completion of a thesis, typed and bound and presented to the library and to the agency for the use of other students and workers, gives him a new and satisfying sense of his achievement as a professional person.

This description of the training movement in the thesis project as primarily a process between the adviser and the student with the focus on the student in his final organization and affirmation of his professional self may seem to leave the supervisor with a negligible role. This is by no means the case. One must state her role first in negative terms to realize fully the sacrifice and the discipline it asks her to maintain. Her stake in the first semester has been deep. She has contributed fully of her concern, of her supervisory activity and skill, in bringing the student through to a point where his casework practice can support a thesis undertaking only now to be obliged to resign him to a new process which will involve him more deeply. The kind and degree of separation this asks of her tends to be overlooked in the responsibility she must continue to carry for his work with his cases and his relation to the agency. She must be prepared to be the bearer of his negative projections and to see the final reward of his ending experience given to another person. Only the experienced supervisor who has weathered the sacrifice and the disappointments not once but many times has found a way to carry the very responsible and often odious part that is hers, not only without interference, but with an identification with his thesis process that can be sustaining and helpful to the student as well as satisfying to herself.

School as well as agency expects responsible practice work

of the student in this final semester and little extra time or allowance is made for the thesis writing. Each year as students struggle with this difficult assignment, thesis advisers question again whether the School really asks the impossible! Each year they find the positive answer in the accomplishment of another class of students and must affirm again their conviction of the essential rightness of this process as a whole, which like all living must always seem too hard at the point where one engages with it fully and deeply.

CHAPTER XIII

THE ESSENTIAL BASIS FOR SUPERVISORY SKILL

In locating this description of the supervisory process in the particular structure of the Pennsylvania School of Social Work, I may seem to imply that I believe this to be the only structure within which this process of learning to help in a professional relationship can take place, and perhaps also that this structure is fixed and static. If this were so, the Pennsylvania School would not be willing to use as supervisors any except its own graduates trained in its own structures. On the contrary, the School welcomes as supervisors of students, graduates of other schools, asking of them only one requirement, that they be willing to engage themselves in working with the Pennsylvania School in its structures in training a student. The School does not minimize the learning that will be involved for a supervisor unfamiliar with this school and has set up a class for beginning supervisors which follows the movement of the first-year student in the time structure of the School year, sustained by supervisor in agency and adviser in the School in a focused relationship. A supervisor in choosing to undertake the training of a student in the Pennsylvania School of Social Work is facing for herself a new learning process.

While the graduate of a different school of social work cannot know in advance all that will be involved for her, she will not attempt it at all unless she knows enough about the Pennsylvania School to make this initial choice for herself of a new learning experience. It goes without saying and is a matter of fact that graduates of other schools trained in the Freudian diagnostic approach to the helping process and who are satisfied with this approach and method of helping will hardly risk involving themselves with the Rankian-functional approach and method, exactly opposite as it is in its basic understanding of the self and its use in professional helping relationships.

As supervisors trained in other schools engage in this class and in this learning process they will undoubtedly ask: but what of the psychological point of view which underlies this functional practice? Can we supervise for the School if we are not taught this point of view *as such?*

There can be no question that the method and practice in use in a helping process rest upon a psychology, an understanding of the nature and organization of the self and of its processes of change and growth in helping relationships. This fundamental psychology determines the way in which help is given and the nature of the structures set up to facilitate and direct the professional helping process. The psychological point of view of this school, as I have said in Part II, derives from Rank's Will Psychology and his understanding of helping processes. Rank's articulation of this psychology in *Will Therapy and Truth and Reality* growing out of his long and intensive therapeutic practice is difficult reading. Its meaning eludes the typical intellectual approach and analysis. Only the student who brings to Rank's writings something more than intellectual effort, some ability to connect with his own inner experience and a sufficiently strong desire and purpose to hold himself to the exploration of and deeper understanding of that experience, can relate to Rank's content in a way which enables him to find in it its valid meanings. The School asks of its students and of its supervisors this effort to find meaning for themselves in some part of Rank's work. Beyond this limited use of his psychology it does not expect its students to go, for the additional study required for a comprehensive and objective evaluation of his contribution to psychological theory and therapeutic method goes far beyond what could be expected in a two-year curriculum in social work.

What, then, is the absolute minimum and essential basis of psychological understanding, the necessary unit of experience, knowledge of which is required of students and supervisors of students to enable them to use the practice of this school in helping processes?

I would say that the essential experience on which rests all ability and skill in helping in a professional process is an experience of change within the self which takes place in relation to a projection of this experience on another person who carries the stability which supports this risk of change. There is no experience so fearful, so threatening as the risk of change in the self, for the natural process of living takes place in relation to external reality and the slightest stoppage in this process which forces the movement of energy back from its outgoing expression on its object into the self disturbs the individual profoundly. The extent to which any living organism can tolerate this moment of interference with its movement is probably very limited. It finds its way to go around, to avoid, to overcome the obstacle. The human being alone, for better or for worse, has developed the capacity to take in this moment of interference with its own movement, to know it and deal with it. He alone can become aware of his own inner experience, can tolerate to different degrees his feeling and emotions of fear and of anger, of love and hatred for the other to whom he is related. But in the experience of natural human relationships in everyday living, the individual controls his inner experience, his love and his hate, even when he seems most at the mercy of the other person. It is he, obviously, who determines by all that is in him what he will feel and how he will feel it. No outside force, personal or impersonal, can wrest this control away from him against his will. The uncertainty, then, that an individual faces when he lets himself in for an experience of change in himself of which he does not hold the control constitutes a risk beyond comprehension or description.

It is precisely this risk of the self that the student who would use himself in helping others must face. On the other hand, it must be admitted that it is possible for a student to go through a two-year training process in a school of social work without actually risking himself in this way, just as it is possible for a patient to go to a therapist and prove that his neurosis is incurable or perhaps bring about some change in his neurosis himself against, or in spite of, the therapist. The rigidly organized, deeply negative, as well as the very creative, personality may succeed in sustaining its organization against the other or independently of the other and may indeed be eminently successful in certain undertakings but is surely disqualified for the development of skill in a helping process where sensitivity and responsiveness to the other person are basic requirements.

It is possible, of course, for an individual to experience change in himself in relation to another in life-giving ways without knowing the process by which change was effected. But if one seeks to make professional use of this experience, it is necessary that it be identified as a time-limited, structuralized unit with a describable beginning, a known focus, and a definite ending in time. Some of the detail of content and process must be open for examination and available for use in subsequent experience.

Here, I believe, one runs up against a fundamental human problem, the problem of holding inner experience, immediate, delicate, and fluid as it is, long enough to examine it, to bestow upon it any conceptual words which will not stultify the living quality of the process. Each individual has a unique relation to his own inner experience and describes it for himself, if indeed he attempts to describe it at all, in terms and images peculiar to himself alone. The passion to share this experience, which surely every individual knows at some moment in his life, may never be realized except in very fragmentary and unsatisfying ways subject to misunderstanding. In a therapeutic process, the individual learns to risk these fragmentary expressions of inner experience, trusting them to be understood for what they are, knowing that what is temporary and misleading today can be added to and corrected tomorrow. If this experience in sharing the inner self and its changing feelings and attitudes is to be more than personally therapeutic, ready for use in professional helping processes, some points of process, of movement and change, must be identifiable in language that has common professional meaning.

In the description of the two-year training process which I have given in this book, I have attempted to give meaning to a few concepts, to identify several points of process to serve as guideposts in this movement in a time-structured relationship. I restate these concepts now in conclusion. First, I have emphasized the concept of function, believing that this concept introduces the precise degree of objectification which makes consciousness of inner process possible and describable. Accepted and understood as the necessary basis of a relationship process, it begins to define responsibilities and roles, to indicate direction, to afford opportunities for partialization and deepening of psychological experience.

When function is accepted by a helping person in a professional relationship, there follows at once an understanding of the second concept to which I have assigned importance—the concept of functional difference. One does not need to go far into his inner experience to be aware of the psychological importance of his feeling of difference from others or look around him to any extent without realizing the problem this difference constitutes in the world today. It is only in a functionally controlled relationship, I believe, that the factor of difference can be truly accepted and affirmed by the helping individual because it has been justified by function. This acceptance of his own difference and the responsibility for the use it engenders at the same time develops an increasing sensitivity to the other's difference and greater freedom to relate to him in this process, always directed to helping the other rather than to an expression of his own impulsive feeling or willing.

I have used the word "yield" to identify the moment in

process when an individual gives up his own inner organization in response to what the other person has injected of his difference. This word merely describes, but in no way explains, the complexity of this little-understood experience, in which the very essence of the possibility of change in psychological organization in relationship resides. The degree of yielding will differ from individual to individual, from a fairly superficial giving in of some point in the outer layer of the resistive, fighting self to a deep inner yielding of the whole self in fundamental trust of the other and of this relationship process. This experience in yielding one's own direction and organization is crucial for one's awareness of the strength and nature of his own will and its projection on the other. It marks a shift in balance in the beginning of a new organization of the forces in the self, a different possibility of balance in relation to the other. The words I have used to mark out the time structure in this process are the everyday words in common usage: beginning, middle or turning point, and ending.

Granted the basic experience in the self, acknowledged as change in a professionally controlled relationship in learning a helping process, the individual has within his grasp not only a characteristic unit of experience upon which he can draw for the enlargement and deepening of his own understanding of relationship process but even more than this. What has been revealed of himself in this heightened moment of living in relationship, of hitherto unacknowledged parts of himself, its possibilities for good and evil, for pain and satisfaction, for destructiveness and creativity, is not limited to an understanding of the professional experience alone, but constitutes a deeper source of connection with the complex, living self and of its expression and projection in all its relationships. The process of change, professionally initiated and limited, becomes an organic growth process of the whole self formed and directed by the unique nature of each individual self. Within the controls and structures of service, supervision, and administration in the social agency, the discovery and expression of the creative self can find almost unlimited opportunity if the individual can accept the responsibility for himself, for the other, and for the process which helping demands.

This concept of the self as a living whole whose complex and manifold expressions can never be analyzed and interpreted but can only be understood as a whole underlies all understanding and skill in helping processes. It is this quality and respect in the understanding extended to the person seeking help or to the student in training that enables him to yield his defenses to the other. The supervisor's essential skill, I believe, stems from this respect for her self and for the other and extends only so far as she can truly take in and comprehend the unique self of the other and accord to that self the right to its difference while holding it to the change which must take place in the learning process.

PART 4

THE GRADUATE IN THE SOCIAL AGENCY

CHAPTER XIV

THE GRADUATE IN THE SOCIAL AGENCY

At the end of this two-year training process, the graduate moves into a social agency as a caseworker and staff member to use the skill that he has learned in service to clients. He expects of the agency recognition of his training in salary and conditions of work that will guarantee a continuance of development for his professional skill. While the sense of strength and independence in the self, the natural reaction to ending training, craves greater responsibility and welcomes the new status of worker in place of student, there is no doubt in the graduate's mind of the need for supervision to help him take on this responsibility. He asks that the supervisor have skill in the helping process that has gone beyond his own, that she be firmly rooted in her knowledge of agency function and structures; he depends on her strength and skill in supervision to hold him to the best use of himself in this, his first agency placement as worker.

The agency and the supervisor who expect the student to come from the professional school a finished product and who overlook the necessity for a new beginning as a worker in an agency make a serious error. Any change in function, in status, requires for any worker, however experienced, a new beginning, a developmental process in defining this difference. Since the dynamics of a beginning process are essentially the same at every level of experience and skill, if a supervisor has learned what it takes to help a student begin in the agency with one case and then with a case load she will know how to help the graduate of the school to begin as a worker. If, as sometimes happens under the pressure of agency emergencies and staff shortages, the supervisor skips this beginning and expects the new worker to identify with agency necessities and take on responsibility for function

141

and total case load too quickly, she will be forced by the worker's reactions to go back over the beginning she has skipped and retrieve her error.

However desirable it might seem at times from the standpoint of more efficient service to clients, there can be no short cut for staff in these processes of identification with the function of the agency and the development of a working relationship between supervisor and worker. Each new worker must struggle as the student does to bring himself and his previous training and equipment into the new situation. He must overassert or withdraw himself, take too much upon himself or too little, in his effort to become established. Some of the negative aspects of this struggle will again be projected onto the supervisor who holds him to this difficult process. In doing this he may seem to repeat the pattern of his early studentship, but this repetition is on another level and he should come more quickly than he did as a student to recognition of these negative projections as his own and to the acceptance of responsibility for them.

As the worker becomes integrated into the agency and moves ahead from one department or job process into another, from giving direct service to clients to supervising, every step in this movement requires the skilled help of supervision in ending one phase of experience and beginning the new, if his relation to his own skill and to the agency as a whole is to be soundly sustained and developed. At the same time, as he moves into agency more responsibly, he seeks a more direct connection with agency as a whole in addition to that maintained through his relation to his supervisor. He seeks a closer connection with administration, opportunities to make effective his ideas about the agency, its service, or its structural organization. He seeks promotion in salary, in recognition of his greater skill and ability to participate in agency development.

It is important to see these needs, not only as legitimate expressions of professional growth, but as the very source of new creative contribution to the agency's life and development. It must be a primary responsibility of the administrator to keep himself sensitive to the need of staff for these opportunities for expression of their creativity in relation to agency, to know through the supervisors where each staff member is in his use of himself in agency, to realize when he is ready for change of function, greater responsibility, or promotion. The administrator must establish, either through himself or an assistant, his own direct lines of connection with each worker, at the time of employment and at every change in agency status. These contacts can carry the developing process of the worker's relation to agency as a whole, his sense of himself as a functioning part in this whole, in a way that goes beyond what is carried between him and his supervisor in the process that concerns his skill in giving agency service. His feeling of himself in relation to the whole will, of course, affect his casework and when it becomes negative must be tackled in supervision; on the other hand, it is valuable for the supervisor to be able to help him to mobilize his feelings of irritation or impatience because he has not been promoted fast enough or given opportunities for committee work, and to take them to the administrator whose function it is to carry responsibility for salary, for status, for the movement of staff members in relation to the agency as a whole. Administration that carries this function sensitively and wisely can, I believe, hold professional staff for many years of service.

While giving full recognition and welcome to the positive creative contribution of a growing professional staff to the agency, the administrator who lacks understanding and conviction of the necessity of negative forces in a growth movement will fail in his ability to deal wisely with his staff relationships. Often, in the large agency, the administrator feels himself cut off from the positive aspects of the service-giving experience of agency and the satisfying experience of supervision and left to carry the burden of setting limits, of enforcing harsh decisions, of standing for hard refusals. It is his job to meet the staff worker who comes to him fresh from a positive evaluation with a supervisor, full of ego aggrandizement, ready for promotion in his sense of himself and his acknowledged capacities. Administration, in its necessity to balance agency needs as a whole, may not be able to offer the supervisory job for which this worker feels himself ready. The worker, on the other hand, has separated himself sharply from his identification with agency and from his role in it, as a natural result of this growth process culminating in a positive ending and evaluation with his supervisor. It devolves upon the administrator then to help him work through this inevitable impulse toward separation from the old situation to a new relation to the agency if he is to stay on without alienation and with a more positive use of himself. How often at this point we see the worker, in his sense of discrepancy between his own needs and agency's recognition and plan for him, decide to leave agency or turn into a demanding, protesting, unprofessional individual full of complaint and pressure! This feeling of alienation may even develop into a more or less fixed antagonism to agency administration which will express itself in little ways or perhaps take itself to the union for support and confirmation.

The worker whose development has been good and who could perhaps well use a promotion constitutes only one kind of staff problem with which the administrator must deal. More difficult to handle may be the worker whose skill has not developed and who must be required, for the sake of the clients who are not getting the service they need, either to leave the agency or to do something more about his failure to use himself helpfully. A point of decisiveness and finality such as this in relation to a worker comes only after the supervisor has tried everything she knows in supervision and has been met by an unyielding refusal.

Such discrepancies between the worker's use of himself, his needs and his contribution, his rate and level of growth, and the agency's evaluation of them and its capacity to absorb and use them must arise again and again between the agency that encourages and supports professional growth and staff members who are developing as individuals while they must also be held as integrally related parts of this organic agency whole. Just as the sense of difference and the need to assert it were seen to be inevitable accompaniments of the student's training movement in the supervisory relationship, so now we must expect to find a similar process in the worker's movement in agency. It is to be expected in even greater degree as the self of the experienced worker, more fully released and more deeply engaged, gathers greater strength both negative and positive in its growth movement.

Necessary and desirable as we know this strength to be in the development of professional skill, valuable as is the release of individual creative expression in the growth of agency itself, what it asks of an administrator to hold these forces in a moving relationship to a whole goes beyond what social workers with few exceptions have been willing to take on themselves. Few supervisors, no matter how far they have gone in the development of supervisory skill, have been willing to go beyond the level and responsibility of the case supervisor to accept the greater responsibility for carrying the direction and sustaining the focus of the agency as a whole. The large agency frequently goes outside of professionally trained staff to seek the administrator who understands administration and management in some field other than social work. In my judgment this encourages and increases the split all too apt to appear between administration and the living processes of the service agency. I believe that only the professionally trained administrator who understands the meaning of a helping process because he has been through it in his own experience and who sees every process in the agency in terms of a basic understanding of change, movement, and growth can carry the function of the agency as it must be carried for the full use and development of professional skill in service to clients. The administrator must carry the function of the agency with a deeper focus in himself than any staff member and with as keen an awareness of how this will be opposed and where difference will be expressed as the worker or supervisor feels in a helping process. His acceptance of differences in staff attitudes as he feels them must be immediate and positive while his ability and strength to maintain the difference of his own function where necessary must be firm and unyielding.

The graduate of the professional school looks to the administrator of the agency for the kind of understanding of his own movement in process that he has experienced in supervision, the same ability to hold firm against his struggle to control. His training has given him a right to expect this. But as he moves into a more responsible relation to agency he must learn to give up his original use of agency as the situation which seemed ideally set up for his own training needs and permit it to exist in its own independent, imperfect reality in process of being created by many forces and relationships. Every graduate, no matter what his intellectual knowledge of the history of social work, must learn for himself to his great astonishment that the social agency is a much older institution than the professional school. Many of the agencies in which these graduates are employed have more than half a century of existence behind them. Membership on their boards of directors has been handed down from one generation in a family to another. The case records of these agencies record devoted, continuous, personal service to clients through the years, the professional help which the graduate of the training school has learned to offer, entering into this record only within the last decade or two. What these agencies symbolize in the community is rooted in old tradition, responsive as it undoubtedly is to new influences. Even the younger, more recently established agencies with less burden of tradition to carry are indigenous in the community where they are established and are defined by the attitudes and interpretation of their boards of directors, by the clients and their experience in using the service, as well as by the professional staff. These traditions and these complex relationships which constitute the living, changing reality of the social agency, the young graduate assails in his belief in the value and importance of professional skill. For all that he has had an experience in process in his own training and understands to some degree the slow rhythm of any process of organic change and growth, he has little patience with and no understanding of the slow rhythm of agency movement. He seizes upon its personnel policies as an area where change is usually needed and puts all his strength, energy, and determination into an effort to make the agency over in respect to these practices.

In this concern with personnel practices, there is a growing tendency among professional social workers to identify themselves with the rank and file in the labor movement and to take on the pattern of the labor contract, the strike, the pressure methods characteristic of the struggle of labor against management. In this struggle, labor feels itself to be right, justified in fighting by every aggressive means to bring about equality in society. It sustains this projection of difference, this conviction of the rightness of its own cause, ends, and methods by a dependence on the sense of likeness within the own group. However closely social work may be in sympathy with the goals of the labor movement—and the elimination of gross inequalities of opportunity is indeed a traditional and cherished goal of social work—if it follows the labor movement in its projection of difference, it repudiates the understanding and use of psychological difference, which is its own unique professional discovery and contribution. A curious phenomenon in the profession today appears in the ability of caseworkers to use their understanding of psychological and functional difference with the finest conscious professional skill in helping relationships with their clients and in supervisory relationships with workers while, at one and the same time, they depart from this understanding and skill and operate on a different psychological and ethical basis in relationships with management and board in the agency. Essential to the casework method in its use of difference is its acceptance and inclusion of the other person's difference, expressed in his feelings, his attitudes, his will, which determines his sense of what is right for him. While always holding to agency service and his own integrity, which constitute the essential difference with which the client must deal, the caseworker never fails to know that it is the client for whom this service is extended, that it is the client who must find his own difference and rightness. With such an understanding and in the use of this method, force and pressure as used in labor relationships have no place in the caseworker's hands.

The passionate intensity with which young caseworkers pursue this identification with the labor movement makes one wonder whether the very degree of individual responsibility and personal discipline which the helping function demands of the caseworker does not bring out this behavior as an inevitable reaction against itself. Perhaps the human being cannot carry this much responsibility for his own difference, for his will to assert and use it, even though this use is in behalf of the other. The guilt for the assertion of difference implying advantage or superiority, an assertion which the helping person must make and sustain, may be compensated for by an identification with the rank and file of labor, the disadvantaged of society. The negative feelings which find expression in the fight for better working conditions and higher salaries may stem too from a deeper source in the internal pressure which social workers must feel in the process of learning to bear these feelings in the self, of learning to sacrifice the impulsive expressions of the personal self in the interest of the client. The common cause of the labor movement gives justification to these feelings and their

projection and affords the relief of identification with a group
where difference can be submerged.

However one may try to understand this relation to the
labor movement, practically and immediately the strain
which it puts on the social agency is serious. Board, administration, and supervisors who carry responsibility for administration are pushed into the camp of the enemy; service
to clients may be interrupted. If this goes too far, the agency
becomes conflicted and torn, and loses the unity of purpose
and wholeness in its structure and organization which is
essential if it is to offer its clients a consistent, helpful service, and the worker is deprived of the agency whole, by
which his difference can be carried.

This problem of conflict between the functional parts of
an organization is certainly not peculiar to social work. In
the large industrial organization, management and working
staff are separated from the beginning in interests, the one
concerned with production and profit, the other with wages
and working conditions. In the small organization or shop
where management is close to staff and includes its interests
and where pride in craftsmanship and in the standards of the
product itself take precedence over mass production and
profit, the organization tends to a unity and wholeness organic in nature as is the unity of the social agency. The
separate forces within contend with each other and are bal-
anced and reunited in a natural, unconscious growth process.
This tendency in the small individual plant today is opposed
by the movement to mergers and bigger and bigger organ-
izations on the part of industry. At the same time the whole
strength of the labor movement stands arraigned against
unity and integration in the individual plant in its determination to make acute and conscious the conflict in interest
between capital and labor, to maintain and organize labor
unity in a whole which takes precedence over the unity in
the individual, separate business or organization.

Any organization, whose primary function is service rather

than profit, must maintain a unity and wholeness within its own structure. It cannot permit its functional parts to be split into separate pieces, each depending for its positive unifying relationship on something outside the organization, with the fight carried in the organization itself. It must believe in the service it offers and all of its effort must be directed to rendering that service more effective, more useful to its clients. Particularly for the social agency, dedicated to the responsibility of helping human beings in need, the belief in the value of that service must be deep and unshakable. Through the long, slow process of interaction between professional staff, board, and clients when held together by a common devotion to the goal of service and a common understanding of the processes by which that goal is expressed, the creation of an organic unity strong and capable of further change and growth can take place.

The dynamic possibilities of the service itself and the life and growth of the agency which extends and sustains the service depend upon the strength and vitality of the opposing psychological forces that contend in separation and unification, in taking and offering help in human relationships. Each individual caseworker, every supervisor and administrator, must accept the difficult discipline of learning to bear within himself and within the agency as a whole the conflict of those forces. Every worker must fight this discipline again and again, must project it onto supervisor and administrator, and will need help in taking this fight back into himself.

On this understanding of positive and negative forces in the self and their projection and struggle in a helping relationship rest the training and skill of the graduate of the professional school as I have described it. This understanding of a helping process is new in professional training. What it asks of the graduates who, as caseworkers, offer this service to clients, of the supervisors who teach it, of the administrator who holds the parts of the agency together, the development and disciplined use of the whole self, is new in human experience. Only longer and more extended use of this understanding and method of helping can determine, not its value—for that is demonstrated—but the willingness of professional workers to make the sacrifice of the personal for the professional, of the self for the other, the difficult discipline which this skill requires of its practitioners.

SELECTED BIBLIOGRAPHY

I

SUPERVISION AND TRAINING

Allen, Frederick H. "Training in Child Psychiatry," *American Journal of Orthopsychiatry*, Vol. XVI, No. 3, July 1946.

Bishop, Margaret E. *The Selection and Admission of Students in a School of Social Work*. University of Pennsylvania School of Social Work, 1948.

Faith, Goldie Basch. "Class Room and Field Work: Their Joint Contribution to Skill" in *Training for Skill in Social Case Work*. University of Pennsylvania Press, 1942.

Lazarus, Esther. "Integration of Supervision with the Total Program of the Agency," *Proceedings* of the National Conference of Social Work, 1947, pp. 251-60.

Levinson, Frances. "The Generics of Supervisory Process," *Jewish Social Service Quarterly*, March 1949.

Reynolds, Bertha. *Learning and Teaching in the Practice of Social Work*. New York: Farrar and Rinehart, 1942.

Reynolds, Rosemary. *Evaluating the Field Work of Students*. Pamphlet. Family Service Association of America, n.d.

Robinson, Virginia P., Editor. *Supervision in Social Case Work*. Chapel Hill: University of North Carolina Press, 1936.

———. *Training for Skill in Social Case Work*. University of Pennsylvania Press, 1942.

Towle, Charlotte. "The Emotional Element in Learning in Professional Education for Social Work," *Professional Education,* American Association of Schools of Social Work, March 1948.

Wessel, Rosa. "Training for Skill in Casework in a School of Social Work," *The Compass*, September 1944.

II

SUPERVISION

Unpublished Theses, Pennsylvania School of Social Work, 1941-48

Baer, Evelyn S. The Specific Aspects of Supervision in a Child Placing Agency. 1943.

Barral, Esther Rosenblum. The Supervisor's Responsibility for the Professional Development of the Untrained Worker in the Public Assistance Agency. 1941.

Burgess, Caroline Bartow. Learning What Is Involved in Helping a Worker Use a Change of Supervisor in Red Cross Hospital Service. 1947.

Clepper, W. Wendell. Training through Supervision in a County Child Welfare Agency. 1943.

Cohen, Frances G. Policy Which Determines Method—Its Validity for the Supervisory Process in a Public Assistance Agency. 1944.

Cole, Jewell. The Significance of Feeling in the Supervisory Process That Is Directed toward the Development of the Public Assistance Worker's Requisite Skill. 1944.

Finkbinder, Roberta. Supervision as the Fundamental Professional Skill in the Administration of Assistance. 1942.

Goldstein, Lillian Isgur. The Role of the Supervisor in Helping a Student Meet Failure in Casework. 1946.

Hayden, Robert Lawrence. Defining the Role of the Case Supervisor in a New Agency. 1947.

Kahn, Margaret. Resolving Worker-Client Impasse within the Supervisory Relationship. 1945.

Kerner, Catherine. An Experiment in Developing Policy in a Public Assistance Agency through Staff Participation. 1944.

King, Julia. Learning to Use the Function of the Supervisor to Help a First Year Student Move through the Anxiety and Resistance Inherent in the Learning Process toward a Responsible Choice of Training for Skill in Social Casework. 1948.

Lankford, Elizabeth. Supervision, the Process Which Determines the Quality of the Service That Agency Extends to Client. 1943.

Logan, Frances Walker. Learning to Work with Others in a Supervisory Relationship. 1946.

Pierce, Marion. The Contribution of Supervision to the Training of Counseling Teachers. 1947.

Rabinowitz, Eve. Relationship: The Third Dimension in Supervision. 1943.

Royer, William E. Learning to Use the Supervisory Relationship to Induct the Untrained Worker. 1947.

Shapiro, Violet R. Helping an Experienced Worker Achieve the Responsibility for Self That Would Enable Her to Move on to Maximum Salary and Student Supervision. 1948.

Sharkey, Harold B. Learning to Use the Supervisory Role in Working with Case Aides in a Private Immigrant Agency. 1948.

Silverman, H. Kay. The Problem Presented to Supervision by the Experienced Worker Who Has Ceased to Develop Professionally. 1944.

Smith, Rebecca C. Some Aspects of Casework and Supervisory Practice in a Family Agency during Wartime. 1944.

Terrell, Harriet Levin. Evaluation as a Clarification of the Place of Worker and Supervisor in Agency. 1941.

Tingley, Ruth. Supervision of a District of a Public Department through the Supervisory Relationship. 1946.

Whitelock, Marjory. The Supervisor's Use of Difference in Initiating Change in the Caseworker. 1943.

Wiggins, Marguerite. Supervision as It Affects Services to Clients in a Public Assistance Agency. 1942.

Wolfe, Lucille. The Use of Probation Period and Status in Supervision of the New Worker in a Family Agency. 1945.

Young, Marechal-Neil. The Contribution of Supervision to the Movement of Junior High School Counselors in Their First Term of School Counseling. 1948.

Zimmerman, Rebecca. The Critical Phases in the Initial Period of Supervising a Worker in a Child Care Agency. 1943.

① Diff in degree in
focus on past
as your present
rec — present

② Diff. in extent to
which Client
believed + expected
to be capable.